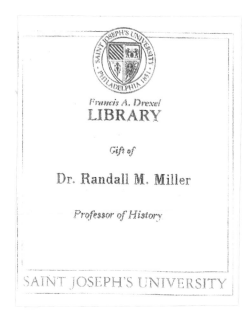

# ENCHANTED AISLES

BY

## ALEXANDER WOOLLCOTT

AUTHOR OF "MR. DICKENS GOES TO THE PLAY"

G. P. Putnam's Sons
New York & London
The Knickerbocker Press
1924

KRAUS REPRINT CO.
Millwood, N. Y.
1975

Library of Congress Cataloging in Publication Data

Woollcott, Alexander, 1887-1943.
    Enchanted aisles.

    Reprint of the ed. published by Putnam, New York.
    1. Theater—United States—Addresses, essays,
lectures.   I.  Title.
PN2266.W56   1975        792'.0973        75-22188
ISBN 0-527-98050-1

*Reprinted by arrangement with The Viking Press, Inc.*

KRAUS REPRINT CO.
A U.S. Division of Kraus-Thomson Organization Limited

Printed in U.S.A.

To
EDNA FERBER

Acknowledgment is hereby made to the editors of *Vanity Fair*, *Scribner's*, *The North American Review*, *Life*, *The New York Times* and *The New York Herald*, in whose columns some of this material originally appeared.

# CONTENTS

## I. ENTHUSIASMS

# ENCHANTED AISLES

I

ENTHUSIASMS

## DE PACHMANN

THE most astonishing, most alive and most infectious dramatic performance given in our town one Autumn week was not that of Miss Eagels in "Rain." No; nor that of Mrs. Fiske in "Mary, Mary Quite Contrary" at the Belasco. It was the astoundingly expressive and utterly enthralling performance which a happy, little, old man named Vladimir de Pachmann gave on a Thursday evening at Carnegie Hall, when, in the almost accidental presence of several thousand passersby, he sat down at a piano and, for two crowded, exultant hours, dwelt with Beethoven, Chopin and Franz Liszt.

Not without cajolery, we had obtained seats so close that it was possible to hear every groan and every chuckle, possible to see every gesture of hand and shoulder, every recorded emotion, however fleet, of one who plays the piano with every last atom of his devoted self. Thus we went home from Carnegie Hall the richer for a stirring and unprecedented experience. It was, therefore, something of a blow to find that in all the newspapers which passed our way the next day, contumely, or at best an amused and patronizing tolerance,

3

was De Pachmann's portion.  The single exception we chanced to note was the altogether human and spirited account of the adventure which Gilbert Gabriel wrote for *The Sun and The Globe*.  But from such usually humane and perceptive fellows as Deems Taylor of the *World* and Lawrence Gilman of the *Tribune* came mostly bricks—projectiles which from their speed and direction suggested to us that the critics had heard De Pachmann play and missed the point.

It is hardly necessary for your correspondent to explain that in such company he would hardly venture an opinion as to whether or not the old man played well. But Mr. Gilman called it "a one man vaudeville show," and we do consider vaudeville within our province. After all, this was a dramatic performance, too. De Pachmann seemed to us to be caressing that piano and to be evoking from it a voice of gold, but then, too, there was Chaplin at that piano, there at times was such brilliantly expressive pantomime as that with which Paul Clerget glorified the Ames revival of "L'Enfant Prodigue." There was *Deburau* himself. Nay, there was *Pierrot* grown old and free and given to talking to the moon.

As every one knows, De Pachmann, with many winks, chuckles, groans and appeals to heaven, keeps up a continuous, murmurous chatter about the music he is invoking. To himself, to the spirits of the dead, to any within range of his half-whispered monologue, he talks about that music, about how it came to be written, how Liszt played it, how he hopes to play it, how beautiful it is, and so on, and so on. It is chatter which only a few can hear distinctly and of which the eccentricity sets the remoter or more woolly witted auditors into a fit of the giggles. If you are nearer you see how the moods of the melody—fear, hope, anger, love, gayety, despair—write themselves on every aspect of his mobile face, in every line of his responsive body. If you are nearer still you can hear enough to know he is now exultant in a free and childlike way at his own astonishing dexterity, now mortified at his own shortcomings, now grateful to whatever god brought the wonder of music into an ugly world.

He is thinking aloud—or, to be more exact, feeling aloud. A difficult Impromptu of Chopin may be before him. He wonders if he will play it well. He prays he will. It will tax his memory, and, after all, he is an old man now, a shrunken old man of seventy-five whose memory is not what it was. But, come, come, De Pachmann! Mere music teachers can memorize. What counts is intelligence. Courage, De Pachmann! "Dear God, help me to play this beautiful music to-night as You meant it to be played when You sent it into the world." Fragments of something like this escaped from the little man as he served at that altar on Carnegie's stage.

Such communicativeness in the world of affairs or on

the concert platform may be an infirmity, but, after all, it is a part of De Pachmann, and one did not come away from Bernhardt's last "Camille" denouncing her for being a grandmother with a wooden leg. It is barely possible that De Pachmann could be made by a grim management to keep his behavior orderly, his face straight, his mouth shut. But probably he would burst. It was possible for the late Ned Harrigan to take his aspiring young son, William, into his troupe and command him for the first six weeks to play every scene with his hands limp at his sides, in order to force the lad to a greater reliance on the expression of the face and the tone of the voice. But one who compelled Duse or Mrs. Fiske to keep her hands at her sides throughout a performance would be inviting an earthquake.

To those sitting further from the stage it may be— nay, it must be—maddening to have the most delicate transitions of the Chopin nocturnes drowned in the empty laughter of giggling neighbors. But it was the whole implication of the more ferocious reviews that these "antics," these "monkeyshines," these "capers" were the tricks and manners of an old showman who was going to attract an audience by fair means or foul. Yet really weren't they rather the candors of an artless and quite simple person who would have behaved in exactly the same manner had the hall been empty and who would have had just as good a time alone with the composers? Many of these "monkeyshines" were prayers, for De Pachmann was not talking to A-2, A-4, A-6, A-8. He was talking to God.

Deems Taylor did not stick it out. He went away in distress, "feeling a little ashamed of caring so much about music in a world where so many excellent people didn't mind a bit what happened to it." Well, that makes two of them, for, though Mr. Taylor's implication was rather to the contrary, we have a suspicion that there was another person in Carnegie Hall that night who cared as much about music as ever man cared since the first note sounded across the void. The other man's name was Vladimir de Pachmann.

.    .    .    .    .    .    .

It was in the hubbub of discussion following De Pachmann's first concert in New York after his long absence that Brother Taylor sat him down and tartly wrote for *The New York World* his notion of how "A Doll's House" would sound if Mrs. Fiske were to play *Nora* in the De Pachmann manner. Just listen to this:

NORA—I have waited so patiently for eight years; for goodness knows I knew very well that wonderful things don't happen every day. *That's a tricky speech.* Then this horrible misfortune came upon me; and then I felt quite certain—*I don't know what's come over that electrician; the lights are awful to-night*—that the wonderful thing was going to happen at last. *My throat's bad again. I must remember that aspirin!* When Krogstad's letter was lying out there—*did you notice that the property man forgot it to-night?*—never for a moment did I imagine that you would consent to accept this man's conditions. *Watch my change of voice in this next speech:* I was so absolutely certain that you would say to him: Publish the thing to the whole world. And when that was done—*how's that for technique?*

HELMER—Yes, what then?—when I had exposed my wife to shame and disgrace? *Can't I say anything but the lines, Minnie?*

NORA—*I should say not! Who's the heroine of this play, anyhow?* When that was done, I was so absolutely certain, you would come forward and take everything upon yourself—*awfully good house to-night*—and say: I am the guilty one.

HELMER—Nora!

NORA—It is a thing hundreds of thousands of women have done.

HELMER—Oh, you think and talk like a heedless child! *You jumped a long speech just there.*

NORA—Maybe. *Oh, Lord, so I did.* But you neither think nor talk like the man I could bind myself to. *My throat certainly is sore to-night.* As soon as your fear was over—and it was not fear for what threatened me, but for what might happen to me—*there aren't many women could get over a parenthesis like that*—when the whole thing was past—*I pray Gott I can remember the rest of this darned speech*—as far as you were concerned it was exactly—*Ibsen showed me how this should be played*—as if nothing at all had happened. Exactly as before I was your little skylark, your doll— *Alex Woollcott thinks I'm the best actress in the world; dear man!*—which you would in future treat with doubly gentle care, because it was so brittle and fragile. *Mon Gott, what a beautiful speech!*—Torvald, it was then it dawned upon me that for eight years I had been living— *I saw Janet Achurch play this scene once; Mon Gott, she was terrible!*—here with a strange man, and had borne him three children—*now watch how I take this climäx*—Oh, I can't bear to think of it! I could tear myself into little bits. *Ah, bravo, Fiske! Bravo!*

# BERNHARDT

IT was to "pauvre Rachel" that Bernhardt's thoughts flew as her boat pulled away from these shores after her first glittering tour more than forty years ago. A generation before that her forerunner in the French theater had, in a humiliating and grotesquely disastrous tour, found us a less hospitable, less civilized and less understanding land and had known the agony of playing her great scenes of tempest and woe to the whirr and rustle of a thousand turning pages, each head in the audience bent earnestly but disconcertingly over a translation of the play. "Pauvre Rachel" and the "Divine Sarah" are in the same company to-day—the illustrious company that lies in Père Lachaise, the sloping crowded cemetery, marooned now in a dreary part of Paris where elevated trains roar by and there is an unending rattle of trucks and trams on the streets all about.

It had been Bernhardt's plan to lie buried in a tomb cut deep into the seawashed rock of her own Belle Ile, that little, white edged island which lies just off the ugly port of Saint Nazaire and which, in the morning sunlight, was the first glimpse of France that greeted the soldiers from America who sailed in the first contingent in the half forgotten excitement of June, 1917. But, in the juggling of her moneys which distracted all her later years, she lost the island, so that, after all, it was to Père Lachaise that Paris carried her. She is in the company not only of Rachel, whose grave is in the older and leafier corner close to the twin tomb of Abelard and Heloïse, but in the company, too, of others who, like herself, had had their day in the theater. Talma is there and Molière. Playwrights like De Musset, Beaumarchais, Oscar Wilde and Scribe; painters like Corot, Ingres, Daubigny, Gustave Doré and David. Dr. Hahnemann is there. So is August Comte and Balzac and Marshal Ney and La Fontaine. It is a great troupe—the company of Père Lachaise.

We saw her in her last June. There she sat in her little, cheerful sitting room up in the musty, frowsy, old house in the Boulevard Pereire, which belongs, they say, to some South American government, but from which, since the day when an infatuated Minister had grandly placed it at her disposal, she had never been ousted. She was resplendent in a dressing gown of white satin with a saucy, fur edged overjacket of blue Indian silk and there were blazing rings on the ancient fingers which now and again adjusted the jacket so that there should always be a good view of the scarlet Legion of Honor badge on her breast. It had taken her

so many years and so much trouble to get it.  Her face
was a white mask on which features were painted, but
no craft of makeup could have wrought that dazzling
smile which lighted the room.  Just as in the glory of
her early years, she had never suggested youth but
seemed an ageless being from some other world, so now,
in her seventy-eighth year, it was not easy to remember
that she was old.

There she sat, mutilated, sick, bankrupt and, as always, more than a little raffish—a ruin, if you will, but
one with a bit of gay bunting fluttering jaunty and
defiant from the topmost battlement.  There she sat, a
gaudy old woman, if you will, with fainter and fainter
memories of scandals, ovations, labors, rewards, in-
trigues, jealousies and heroisms, notoriety and fame,
art and the circus.  But there was no one in that room
so young and so fresh that this great-grandmother did
not make her seem colorless.  She was nearly fourscore
years of age and had just finished a long, harassing
season.  But she was in no mood to go off to the shore
for her rest until she had adjusted her plans for this
season.  There were young playwrights to encourage
with a pat on the head, there were scene designers and
costumiers to be directed, there were artists to be inter-
viewed and there was need of some sort of benign
intervention in behalf of a new play struggling along in
her own theater.

Above all, there were plays to be selected for the following season and, if none appeared, then there were playwrights to be lectured or cajoled into writing them for her. She had one hand on the younger Rostand, son of the finest imagination harnessed by the French theater in half a century, son of the Rostand who had written for her the very play that was halted at the Théâtre Sarah Bernhardt in the Place du Chatelet the night she died. This son of his, surely, could be depended on. And in case he couldn't she had her eye on the younger Guitry. Indeed, she had just had herself carried around to his house and had dazzled him all through luncheon for no other purpose. Out of this was born a project for a play about "Adam and Eve," which Sacha Guitry, reluctant but helpless, forthwith began to write. Bernhardt would play *Eve*, of course, and the elder Guitry, *Adam*. This prospect, at first encounter, seemed alarming and the author was questioned. Surely, he was not thinking of writing for them the drama of Eden nor blandishing Bernhardt into thinking that she could suggest *Eve* before the Fall.

"I am not a fool," he replied, tartly. "When my play opens, *Eve* is 650 years old."

"And *Adam?*"

"*Adam* is 750 years old."

"But how did you know there was just that difference?"

"He read it," put in Guitry, *père*, "*dans la Gazette de Milton*."

And America. Of course, she was full of shrewd questions about America. She wanted to know what new playwright might be dug up there, what this O'Neill was like and if business was good at the box offices in New York. She asked after *la petite Taylorrr*, whose great success, "Peg de mon Cœur," was even then playing in Paris and who had had, Bernhardt always knew, *beaucoup de talent*. She was planning, she confessed, to visit us in the winter.

"Not a long tour this time," she added a little ruefully and then went on in the exceptionally earnest tone of one who expected to be doubted, "I am too old and too frail to undertake one of those exhausting tours. Not a long one this time. Just Boston, New York, Philadelphia, Baltimore, Washington, Cleveland, Chicago and a few places like that." This program was proffered without a suggestion of humor. She meant it. She was magnificent.

There are many portraits of her, none lovelier nor more discerning than the slim, serpentine Claretie painting, so often reproduced. The original hung at the far end of the long, ground floor salon in the Boulevard Pereire, a room rich in the elegance of the eighties and crowded like the Cluny Museum with relics of a past civilization, a thousand and one trophies of triumphs from Moscow to Valparaiso. But there is no portrait probably which so catches the essential thing in her as the word portrait by Rostand which Forrest Izard has reproduced in his excellent book, "Heroines of the Modern Stage." It runs thus:

"All these things that I have known only in the telling—all these journeys, these changing skies, these adoring hearts, these flowers, these jewels, these embroideries, these lions, these one hundred and twelve rôles, these eighty trunks, this glory, these caprices, these cheering crowds hauling her carriage, this crocodile drinking champagne—all these things, I say, astonish, dazzle, delight and move me less than something else I have often seen: this—

"A brougham stops at a door; a woman enveloped in furs jumps out, threads her way with a smile through the crowd attracted by the jingling bell on the harness and mounts a winding stair; plunges into a room crowded with flowers and heated like a hothouse, throws her little beribboned handbag, with its apparently inexhaustible contents, into one corner and her bewinged hat into another, takes off her furs and instantaneously dwindles into a mere scabbard of white silk, rushes onto a dimly lighted stage and immediately puts life into a whole crowd of listless, yawning, loitering folk; dashes forward and back, inspiring every one with her own feverish energy; goes into the prompter's box, arranges her scenes, points out the proper gesture and intonation, rises up in wrath and insists on everything being done over again; shouts with fury; sits down, smiles, drinks tea and begins to rehearse her part; draws tears from case hardened actors who thrust their enraptured heads out of the wings to watch her; returns to her room, where the decorators are waiting, demolishes their plans and reconstructs them; collapses, wipes her brow with a lace handkerchief and thinks of fainting; suddenly rushes up to the fifth floor, invades the premises of the astonished costumier, rummages in the wardrobes, makes up a costume, pleats and adjusts it; returns to her room and teaches the figurantes how to dress their hair; has a piece read to her while she makes bouquets; listens to hundreds of letters, weeps over some tale of misfortune, and opens the inexhaustible little clinking handbag; confers with the English perruquier; returns to the stage to superintend the lighting of a scene, objurgates the lamps and reduces the electrician to a state of temporary insanity; sees a super who has blundered the day before, remembers it and overwhelms him with her indignation; returns to her room for dinner; sits down to table, splendidly pale with fatigue; ruminates her plans; eats with peals of Bohemian laughter; dresses for the evening performance while the manager reports from the other side of the curtain; acts with all her heart and soul; discusses business between the acts; remains at the theater until after the performance and makes arrangements until 3 o'clock in the morning; does not make up her mind to go until she sees her stage manager respectfully endeavoring to keep awake; gets into her carriage; huddles herself into her furs and anticipates the delights of lying down and resting at last; bursts into laughter on remembering that some one is waiting to read her a five act play; returns home, listens to the piece, becomes excited, weeps, accepts it, finds she cannot sleep, and takes advantage of the opportunity to study a part. This is the Sarah I have always known. I never made the acquaintance of the Sarah with the coffin and the alligators. The only Sarah I know is the one who works. She is the greater."

Of this passion and capacity for work—what Shaw in his essay on Cæsar describes as "the power of killing a dozen secretaries under you, as a life or death courier kills horses"—the wanderer back stage in our own theater will find some stray examples. Maude Adams had it—a tireless general. Margaret Anglin has it. And Jane Cowl. Bernhardt had it supremely, and even as a sick and crippled woman of seventy-eight she could do more work any day than half the inert young people who litter up the French theater as they do ours. It has been said that she died in harness. That expression of a plodder overtaken by death is inadequate for so gallant, so defiantly twinkling an exit. She was a boat that went to the bottom with its orchestra playing gayly. In her final year she was aflame with that spirit which lighted the despondent blackness of the North Sea one ghastly and terrifying night when a transport carrying some American doughboys to the French battlefields was sunk many miles from shore. They went over the side into the rowboats, not chanting in the approved heroic vein but humming with incorrigible and facetious cheerfulness: "Oh, boys, say, boys, where do we go from here?"

# MADAME COCAUD

HERE he was back in France—back in Paris, and idling pleasantly at one of those sidewalk cafés where you can sit all day and watch the world stream by.

When he sailed from home, it had been in his mind that he would make this trip something of a pilgrimage, that he would tramp once more alone the La Ferté road where first he had watched the Marines going in, find again the Maxfield Parrish forest where the tattered but triumphant infantry fell back for breath after the smash under Soissons, pay an humble visit to the old friend and great priest who kept the faith during the long ordeal of St. Mihiel, nor turn back (as once another half-hearted runaway had done) at Varennes, but push on to explore the new life at each crest and ravine of the Argonne he knew so well.

Above all, he would seek out Savenay, that little Brittany village where he had been stationed for so many months that the very silhouette of its gaunt cathedral and the very color and lullaby sleepiness of its slow-revolving windmills would make a fond reunion. All these things it had been in his mind to do. Yet his two months' stay in France was almost spent and he had done none of them—or done few of them, and that cursorily.

Why? he wondered. Something was missing. What? He, at least, was not one of those varnished tourists who seemingly had expected each group of Frenchmen to welcome them wildly as the first troops of 1917 were welcomed, and so, perforce, went home in sulks. Served them right. But something *was* missing. Perhaps if a finer use had been made of the victory the unquestioning troops had forged, the old scenes of their sacrifice would have called him now more urgently. Maybe his was a mere nostalgia for the lost companionship, a feeling that he could not make the old hikes alone, nor with uncopmrehending strangers. Not that a reluctance to leave the Café Napolitan needs, *per se*, a subtle explanation.

And yet—well, it *was* an uncomfortable thought that all his happy anticipations, all his eager expe ations, all the rendezvous he had made during the fighting, were to be dropped as the mere phantoms of a passing mood, so easily dispelled, so soon forgotten. Surely there must be some continuity, some stamina to his fond desires. One thing he could still do. One thing he need not weakly forfeit to the inertia of the moment. One thing he might carry out to forestall all subsequent regrets. He would at least go back to Savenay.

There was no time to lose. Another week would find him calculating, with furrowed brow, in shillings instead of francs. Another fortnight and he would be toiling up the gangplank at Southampton, tired and homeward bound. If he were going to Savenay, he must start next morning.

So the next morning—it was a Sunday— found him on the platform of the Gare d'Orsay at the incredible hour of seven, armed with a ticket that had cost him about seven times the price he paid when he was one of several million infrequently appreciative public charges. Soon he was tucked in his compartment, a section filled to the brim with bags and bundles and bourgeoisie. It was a sweltering day, yet he knew from their expressions, from the very shape and quality of their luggage, that it would be idle to suggest that the window be opened even a little way.

Air-tight, hot, crowded, grimy—and Savenay ten hours away. Why, in the name of common sense, had he ever quit Paris? What, in the name of human nature, did he expect these lean Bretons to say to him? Most of them would not remember him at all. And why should they? Old Madame Richard, who had thrashed the life out of his weekly shirt at the village *lavoir;* old Madame Lefeuvre, whose booming voice had always been raised in the proud boast that she never used grease in cooking; scornful little Clare, who had served chocolate in the *patisserie* for the insatiable

Americans and had developed there the colorable conviction that they were a species of chocolate soldier—they might remember him. But what of it? Would anyone be glad to see him?

Madame Cocaud, perhaps. Yes, Madame Cocaud, if she were still alive. And, as he drowsed off, his memories staged once more the smoky old buvette, hung with festoons of sausages and with copper kettles innumerable. There, since her widowhood, had Madame Cocaud served the drinks when once a week market day would bring a strange pageant of Breton folk to Savenay and transform the gray square of the *Mairie* into a chattering, fluttering county fair. There, since the black morning when the Government reported tersely and with mimeographed sympathy that her son had been killed at the front, she had dwelt alone, a sleepless and a haunted woman. The neighbors shook their heads, and vowed that poor Mother Cocaud's mind was affected, and avoided her. Then one scorching day in 1917, an American had clattered up to the buvette, put his head in the door, and roared for food. She protested that hers was no restaurant, and he started to go, but, obeying some sudden impulse, she beckoned him back, put a few fresh twigs on the open fire, and bent over a pan that soon produced a supper of extraordinary savor. It was eaten with gusto and was watched over from the shadow of the kitchen by an old woman who, now and again, would lift her apron to her eyes.

That was the beginning of an unofficial American mess which was crowded to suffocation morning, noon and night for two years, until the last boatload of the A. E. F. shoved off for home. Somehow, Madame Cocaud knew that in feeding these young strangers she would find peace,—knew, in a way which satisfied something within her, that, in comforting and cheering them, she would be pleasing her lost son.

What plates of *crêpes*, what pans of Breton sausage, what jars of jam, what cellars of wine vanished in those two years! Which of the boys paid, and how many sneaked away without paying anything, she never knew. She asked only that there be enough funds to keep the supplies moving. She charged so little and her price scale was so sketchy. You would gorge yourself for hours and clamor for your check only to be waved aside, and told to come back another time and settle when she was less busy. If you protested with mock solemnity that you might never come back, she would make a transparent pretense of figuring on a morsel of paper and then, with a comically unsuccessful effort to look severe and commercial, she would emerge with some such absurd charge as three francs.

This utter failure on her part to appreciate the financial opportunities offered by the passing of the crusaders was a source of considerable bewilderment and no little annoyance to her neighbors. They pointed out to her that in time the Americans would be gone, that then the ancient quiet would fall on the village, and that she would have no fortune put away for the after years.

"On whom would I spend it?" asked Madame Cocaud.

The pilgrim would not soon forget that look which used to come into her face when the soldiers ordered to the front came in to kiss her goodbye. Madame Cocaud had a thousand sons in the war. Surely she would remember the least of them, would have a welcome for the meanest of her subjects.

He was thinking of her now and smiling as the train pulled in to Savenay.

It was strange to see the station, once so alive with jostling troops, now quiet and empty. A few folk straggled from the train across the fields. The hill-road to the village square stretched hot and white and steep before him. As he plodded up, he wished devoutly that he had not come. Only one trace of the A. E. F., that was, greeted him as he climbed. It was a little pointing sign which read: "To the American Cemetery."

He dropped his bag at the Hotel of the Green Oak, laid claim to a six-franc room for the night (he wanted to leave on the next train but it would be pusillanimous not to stay till morning) and walked out towards what had been the American hospital.

Here and there along the road, a shopkeeper came out and saluted him cordially but vaguely. It was interesting to find young folk in the street, knots of loitering Willie Baxters as you might find them in any Gopher Prairie of a Sunday afternoon. There had been none in the old days, but now the war was over.

The hospital was gone. The ruddy slanting sunlight fell across the fields where acres of tents and barracks had stood, all of them gone now, even the theater that was built with such energy by its prospective patrons. Still standing, however, was the stone school-house which had been its nucleus, now a school once more, with all the luxurious American plumbing piously torn out and scrapped lest the young idea be softened by too much new-fangled comfort.

There, in a quondam squad-room, where he himself remembered sleeping for a time, there were traces of school-work, scrawled blackboards and all the débris of a class in Molière. At least the bits of paper left lying on the desks indicated that the teacher had been lecturing (tepidly, perhaps) on the sins of "*L'Avare.*" With something of a start, he discovered that the notes had been taken on the back of old American court-martial papers. On the piece he held in his hand, he read the fragment of an indictment which accused (doubtless with justice) one he had known of having gone A. W. O. L.

Here was reconstruction with a vengeance. There was in it something of the lilt of the rhythm of history. He had felt its thrill before, once when he saw German prisoners filling in the trenches around Rheims, again a year later when he had heard the machines threshing in the wheat at Belleau Wood, and only just the other day, when high in the French Alps, at the blazing, blinding electrical forges of Ugines, he had seen the armored turrets of crippled tanks and the rusty cases of a million shells being melted and recast into the tools and machinery of peace.

It was getting late. As he started down the road leading back into the town, he could see ahead of him on the right the jaunty sign of the *patisserie*. He vividly remembered how great was the quantity and variety of cakes it had been possible to wash down with chocolate or *vin ordinaire* during the hour before taps— such variety and such delicacy as no trays of French pastry ever evinced in America. Once he had tried to explore the low-ceilinged kitchen where they were fashioned, only to have the scandalized *patronne* drag him hastily from the threshold. Why, even she dared not cross it. She might employ a famous Breton pastry cook, but, by a law of his guild as old and as strong as Chartes Cathedral, she might not get near enough to him to learn the secrets of his art.

The now cheering pilgrim remembered, too, one drizzling night in the late summer of '17, when the newly arrived Americans found the young *patronne* weeping helplessly over her two-weeks' old son. Her husband was at the front, there were no doctors within many miles, and she was left alone and frightened with a baby whom a clumsy and stupid midwife had blinded at birth. He remembered how the puzzled Americans had carried her off hopefully to where a famous American surgeon, destined for big work in France, was billeted while his orders loitered, how, in two weeks, her boy could see as well as you, and how always thereafter the Americans had a staunch friend at the *patisserie*—that, too, he remembered.

That is why he was sure now that she would be glad to see any of the old crowd. And he was not mistaken. It was not long before the pilgrim was seated in the shop, with the greatly-expanded youngster on one knee and a plate of pastry on the other, while Madame poured steadily from a dusty bottle of Madeira and showered him with questions as to the whereabouts and health of the doctor who had given back her boy's eyes—beautiful eyes, now, and as big as saucers.

She was somewhat taken back when her guest, in his decadent civilian state, paused far short of the eighteen cakes she had recalled as his wartime record. He protested that he must save some room for one of Madame Cocaud's dinners.

"Oh, I am glad you are going there," the little *patronne* assented eagerly. "She is so lonely now. It has been hard for her these days, when all the boys that had been his schoolmates and companions, have come rattling home from the war. To sit alone in your shop and hear the shouts and the laughter when your neighbor's son comes home—that is not easy." There was the ghost of a fear in her eyes as she reached then for her own boy and smoothed out the tousle of his hair.

When, a few moments later, he stood at the threshold of Madame Cocaud's shop, he knew he had come to the end of his little journey. It was a heart-warming reunion, in which one white coif became sadly disarranged. She wanted to ask after twenty men at once and, at the same time, she felt she must begin cooking for the one at hand without loss of time. Almost instinctively, as she rattled on, her hand reached for her frying pan. She did not ask him what he wanted. She knew and set to work contentedly on a mess of *crêpes et saucisses*. She laid no place for him in the gloomy outer room, but cleared his old one at the little table in the kitchen corner, so near the hearth that it was never outside her range as a juggler to flip her cakes from the fire to the table.

A strange and unfamiliar maid hovered on the outskirts of these proceedings. What had become of the old one, the shy, quiet girl who would never engage in even the mildest banter with the hurrying Americans, nor appear with the other natives at the occasional band concert at the hospital? Once Madame Cocaud had tried to beguile her to such a concert, which she herself was dreading because she knew she would be overcome (as, indeed, she was) when they reached the

*Marseillaise.* But the girl had been too afraid of some criticism from the family of her betrothed, who was at the front and might hear that she was gadding about with the Americans.

"And did the boy come back?"

"Oh yes," said Madame Cocaud, "he came back. But, after she had waited five years for him, he married someone else."

This seemed very tragic.

"And the girl, did it hurt her deeply? Was she——"

"Oh, yes, she was inconsolable, quite inconsolable."

"Did she—did she—" he trailed off apprehensively.

"Oh, yes," said Madame Cocaud cheerfully, "she married someone else, too."

Then, as the coffee came on, and a great medley of liqueurs from all manner of strange, squat bottles, she delved into her desk and emerged with an armful of letters and Christmas cards and postals, all from America, a curious assortment of penmanship, from the nice chirography of some remote librarian to the painfully achieved superscription by one infrequently given to the habit of writing. They were all affectionate greetings from her lost Americans, some in earnest French, some in English, some in a fantastic blending of the two. She did not know how to answer them, did not know, indeed, from whom any of them had come. She could only keep them in her desk to be taken out from time to time and held in her lap. The two spent an hour trying to identify the senders. He suggested lightly that she take a page advertisement in an American magazine to acknowledge them, and he had to devote considerable enegry to dissuading her from the notion.

"And here," she said with a twinkle in her eye, "here is something that came yesterday."

So saying, she unfurled a deal of paper and string and brandished therefrom a formidable carving set, which had spent six months seeping through the *douane*. An inclosed card identified the gift as coming from one who had been a private in the A. E. F. and who was now resident in Newark, N. J. She shook her head helplessly, for it is not by the names that she remembers them all.

"I think I know who he is," she confided in a whisper, as though it seemed hardly fair to let the old walls know. "It's a boy who borrowed my carving knife one night and lost it."

They carried the stack of American mail back to the rickety *escritoire* and stuffed it away. There were two other bursting cubbyholes alongside. He pointed questioningly to the first of them.

"They are all the letters about my son," she explained, eyeing them askance. "Letters from the Government, from monument-makers, from dealers in *deuil*, from the school where he studied, from the university where he lectured, from the people in London with whom he stayed when he lectured there. He was a lecturer on peace, Monsieur. *Quelle ironie!*—The letters are all here. See, I have never opened them."

And she darted a frightened look at him, as though she feared he would propose their being opened and read at once. He shifted hastily to the other collection. "And these?"

Whereat she chuckled gleefully and her kindly face— it is the kindliest face in all the world—wrinkled with the quizzical amusement of her famous smile. The A. E. F. justified its existence when, even for a little time, it brought back Madame Cocaud's smile.

"Those," she announced, "are all the letters and threats and warnings from the tax-office inquiring about my excess profits during the war. They've heard somewhere—we all have neighbors—that for two years this was a tremendous restaurant. And now they want a part of the loot. I told them I made no money from the Americans. But what tax-collector would ever believe that? They've asked me now to make out a statement of receipts and disbursements for each day of the war."

And Madame Cocaud, who had often collected only from those who pursued her with insistence that she charge them something, laughed till her white coif shook. But what had she said in reply? Why, she had suggested to the tax-collector that, if he was in such desperate straits, he might go to the war-office and draw the insolent, impious money which was her legal due because her son had been killed for France. For herself, she would never touch a sou of it.

The thought of Madame Cocaud being harried as a profiteer was too much for the visitor. As he uprooted himself at midnight, he asked for his bill. "Oh, you'll be here for breakfast," said she, up to her old tricks. So after breakfast next morning—a very tureen of coffee, and such coffee!—he asked again. "But you will be here for lunch," she suggested, with a baffled look in her eyes. No—see: here was his bag all packed. He was going straight from her door to the cemetery, and then, cutting across the fields, he would catch the morning train back to Paris.

"Ah, then," she said, "I must say goodbye. I couldn't be happy if you went away thinking of this as a tavern where you paid like some stranger. This is your home in Brittany."

So she kissed him on both cheeks, and the memory of her standing in the doorway, to watch him as he crossed the square, was with him an hour later as he clambered aboard the Paris train, put his feet up, covered his face with a copy of *Le Phare*, and settled back to drowse his way to the Gare d'Orsay, while the thump and rattle of the wheels took up a refrain which seemed to say "Glad-you-came, glad-you-came, glad-you-came." There were overtones, too. Over and above the rhythm, there broke clear and satisfying and curiously sad the sound of a page turning in the history of his life.

# NEYSA McMEIN

SOMETHING of the emergence of Neysa McMein, as an artist and a portrait-painter to be reckoned with, has proceeded unobserved and unchronicled, much as a ship can loom suddenly out of a fog. It has taken many onlookers unawares—onlookers who have been distracted from a scrutiny of her work by their amused or annoyed or delighted contemplation of the artist as a person. Just as the full quality of Heifetz's playing might not focus attention completely if he were eight feet tall, so there are plenty of folk in this country who can hardly keep their eyes on the mere work of so glamorous and eventful a lady as Neysa McMein.

Because she has often allowed her pastels to be reproduced by thrifty processes that drain them of half their color and more than half their character; because she will cheerfully draw for a department store, or a soap-maker; because the newspaper reports of her judging beauties at Coney Island, or playing tunes and singing horribly for the wounded soldiers, or opening a new movie house in Toronto, or swimming impromptu in the Marne, arouse suspicions either that she lacks the apocryphal virtue called dignity (which is quite true) or is a schemer for publicity (which is not true at all)— because of all these things it is sometimes too hastily assumed that she can't be a serious and important artist.

"Look at all the things she does!" they say, "—and all the people that swarm and swirl about her. Why, she can't even have time to work."

To which mystery there is really no explanation, except to say first that she is one of those fated persons to whom, and near whom, the most bizarre and nightmare things are always happening. And to say next that she is also one of those amazing beings for whom the day is forty-eight hours long. When she turns out her light at night, she smiles in the joy that another day is coming and, to gather strength for it, she sleeps the fathomless sleep of one buried deep, deep in warm, protecting sand. Her secret is an insatiable, childlike appetite for life—and for the Neysa McMeins of this world, every night in the year is Christmas Eve. The next day may hold an invitation to go on a specially chartered ship to the Orient or a summons to Boston, where she will be permitted to sit humbly at the side of Sargent's easel. Or the White House may send for her. Any day of hers might have all three excitements, and yet the event that would leave the glow at her heart as she snapped out the light at night would be rather the memory of the coal-truck driver who, jammed in the traffic next her

car that afternoon, had leaned over and roared jovially:
"Hello, there, Neysa!" He had known her in the
A. E. F.

From the day when she first came to New York—
Marjorie Moran McMein, of Quincy, Illinois, who
docilely changed her name because some seeress had assured her in sibylline accents that it would bring her luck
—from the early pre-war days when her first covers were
appearing on the news-stands, the work had its present
salient characteristics, honesty and vitality. Each
girl of hers was a real girl, salty with actuality. Here,
for once, was a painter of women who used no stencil.
And to each had been imparted something of her own
abounding joy in just living.

Then, during the last two years, the shift has been
made from mere decoration to the greater exactions
and greater satisfactions of authentic portraiture. The
same period has marked her first experiments in oil.
Her portraits of Ralph Barton, Janet Flanner and
Dorothy Parker are in oil. To my inexpert eye, they
seem admirable, but when a celebrated art critic closes
one eye, sighs deeply and predicts that in a hundred
years art students will be sent to this or that sketch of
hers to learn how a neck should be painted, I have been
carried beyond my depth and, to judge from her own
wide-eyed astonishment, beyond hers, too.

It is difficult for the sober, mincing people of the world
to believe that fine art can take form and life in as turbu-

lent a spot, as crowded, as entertaining and as happy-go-lucky a salon as Neysa McMein's studio. At all hours and at all seasons, there is hubbub there, and many artists would as soon set up their easels in the Grand Central Terminal. In all New York, there is no place quite like it.

The spot itself is a bleak, high-ceilinged room, furnished by the processes of haphazard accumulation. Its decoration ranges from a Briggs strip, torn out of the morning's paper and pinned askew on the wall, to an original Drian, respectfully framed. That splash of vivid color on the screen is a shawl sent by David Belasco and that stretch of gray-green fabric on the wall is a tapestry which she herself bought in Paris and bore home in triumph only to find that the greater part of it had come from the looms way back in the dim days of 1920.

The population is as wildly variegated. Over at the piano Jascha Heifetz and Arthur Samuels may be trying to find what four hands can do in the syncopation of a composition never thus desecrated before. Irving Berlin is encouraging them. Squatted uncomfortably around an ottoman, Franklin P. Adams, Marc Connelly and Dorothy Parker will be playing cold hands to see who will buy the dinner that evening. At the bookshelf Robert C. Benchley and Edna Ferber are amusing themselves vastly by thoughtfully autographing her set of Mark Twain for her. In the corner, some jet-bedecked dowager from a statelier milieu is taking it all in, immensely diverted. Chaplin or Chaliapin, Alice Duer Miller or Wild Bill Donovan, Father Duffy or Mary Pickford—any or all of them may be there. In Paris, they say of the *terrasse* of the Café de la Paix that if you sit there long enough you will see everyone you know. If you loiter in Neysa McMein's studio, the world will drift in and out. Perched on the stool is a delighted model, trying hard to keep her face straight; and if the work is in oil that day, perhaps some older artist may be watching, amused and exasperated at the sight of this woman doing instinctively the things it takes the plodders so many years to learn.

Standing at the easel itself, oblivious of all the ructions, incredibly serene and intent on her work, is the artist herself. She is beautiful, grave and slightly soiled. Her apron is a shabby, streaked remnant of a once neat garment. Her fair hair, all awry, is discolored from an endless drizzle of pastel dust. Her face is smooched with it. She itches to edge one of the pianists to the floor and join the concert herself. The poker game tempts her. But it is not until the daylight has dwindled to dusk that she comes wandering around the easel and drops into a chair, dog-tired but sociable. Indeed, she brings to the party the kind of whole-hearted laughter for which your true comedian will work till he drops. Few persons can tell a story better, but unlike so many who have that gift, she can listen, too. She listens with all her might, which, as those know who have sat at the feet of Mrs. Fiske, is half the art of acting and almost the whole secret of good manners.

What would surprise the people to whom **the** word studio has faint connotations of debauchery, is the homely, neighborly flavor which circumstances and the quality of this woman have imparted to this crazy one of hers. In its casualness and its informality, it has the accent of one of those ugly, roomy, hospitable homes on the edge of a small town, where the young folk are always running in and out. You can almost hear voices calling across the fence, almost catch the aroma of fresh bread sifting from the kitchen.

The sight of Neysa McMein, absently trotting next door in her painting-apron or sitting hatless on the steps to waylay the catnip man in behalf of her beloved Persian, does seem, somehow, to take the curse and the chill off the biggest of cities. She has made a small town of New York.

# DUSE

## I

WHEN the golden curtain of the Metropolitan had fallen after the final act of "The Lady from the Sea," it was Duse who came before it, holding in her still eloquent hands a single white rose from all the gardens for miles around which had been pillaged to do her honor. At her feet the big audience stood and cheered and those of us who must run from every play to a typewriter had to fight our way through aisles which looked as though they would be blocked for hours on end. Our task was the more pressing and the more difficult because all this was the finale of an evening that was at once a play, a reunion, a tribute and a legend come true.

What, in the baldest terms, had taken place in that theater? Well, it was a performance by a nondescript company with forlorn scenery—a performance in Italian of a Norwegian romance that was no great shakes when it was new in its own land and that had never been able to hold its place when shouldered off the stage by the really great plays its author wrote before and after.

It is a romance of two men's struggle to possess a somewhat sedulously mystic lady, and in this company the rôle of the desired *Ellida* was taken by a frail, white haired old woman, who would resort to nothing of paint or wig to hide the wastage which woe and pain and the years had wrought.

Yet if ever any one in the world earned the right to carry on her banners the device which Bernhardt bore —the jaunty and gallant *"Quand-Même"*—that right was Duse's that night. For her performance of *Ellida Wangel* was among the few truly and exhilaratingly beautiful things which we have seen in our time. One who had to wait until far into the twentieth century to see her whom the world called the greatest actress of the nineteenth left the Metropolitan with the feeling that he had never seen any human being of such luminous and transcendent beauty.

Furthermore, it may be doubted if that beauty was clearer or more startling in that day long past when, at sixteen, Eleanora Duse played *Juliet* in Verona. For it is a beauty of line and motion and spirit which the years cannot touch and which can never have had anything of the earthly in it. Twenty and thirty years ago all the scribes of Paris and Rome and London and New York wrote lyrically of "Duse of the beautiful hands." And one guessed from their writings that all those alchemists from Moscow to Manchester, who had been stirring the mortar from which truth should rise, were merely seeking a formula for something that one woman in Italy knew by instinct.   It was something the fairies had whispered in that third class Italian railway train in which Duse was born one October day sixty-four years ago when the family troupe was on the move.

But all written records of a playgoer's memories tell little, and we never knew till our own eyes testified that Duse was beauty in motion—that not her hands alone but every line of her was like thrilling and aching music become animate.   When she moves across the stage it is as though the loveliest sculpture you had ever seen were come magically to life before your eyes.   She is *right* as the Winged Victory is right—as inexplicably and as satisfyingly.   Only once before in our wanderings among the theaters had we seen this instinct thus embodied.   That other player happens to be a clown. His name is Charles Chaplin.

It ought, perhaps, to be made clear that this was Duse in her own person who was so thrilling and so startling.   It was not, by any means, Ibsen's own *Ellida Wangel*—though, if this had been a normal stage and the play had been told in a tongue we knew, it might have been.   Of the Duse who can enter into and become part of a perfect company and who could give full and actual life to some imagined character, we who saw her first at the Metropolitan in 1923 knew nothing when that stirring night was over.

In the inch and the moment that remained it could

be recorded that for once in a way at the Metropolitan the last moments of the program were not scuffled out of existence by the flight of the audience. Also that a list of who was there would fill two columns and make, in booklet form, a handy reference to Who's Really Who in New York. Also that the actor who played the *Stranger*, Memo Benassi, was magnificent. And that at the back of the auditorium, where the faithful stood (some hearing a good deal and some not hearing a word), the imperial Morris Gest might have been seen looking as though the more than $30,000 paid in at the box office for this one performance constituted a not unpleasant feature of the evening.

It was, as a matter of fact, the largest taking for a single commercial performance in the history of the American theater. This was paid to one who, when she first came here in the fulness of her youth and beauty, played to row on row of empty benches. But that was thirty years ago. Since then she had become a legend. That night some of us knew why.


II


The matinée of "Ghosts," which Eleonora Duse and her company from Rome gave at the Century, threw some light on the bafflingly contradictory reports which had preceded the Italian tragedienne from London. Those who saw her one day and those who saw her another told such different stories, and it seems probable that, more than most players, she varies with the tide of her health and spirits.

In all that befell there was much less elation than in that flaming first performance at the Metropolitan the week before. It was an astounding being who swayed with the woe of *Mrs. Alving* and bent to the gusts of mischance which blow upon that most unhappy lady. But it was a frailer and an older being, less ringing of voice more subdued and more fumbling of touch, more weighted down by the shawl that catches and underscores the gracious beauty of her walk.

Not that one need question two different audiences to hear two answers to the mystery of Duse. One man will see on the stage only a fragile, rueful old woman, moving haggard and uncertain through the mazes of an alien play. The man sitting next him will see eloquence suddenly endowed with three dimensions, will see it with the kind of pang only the loveliest and most ghostly strain of Debussy can give him. The two cannot argue. Duse is undebatable.

The audience, which packed the Century from cellar to dome, was harried by the constant prattle of the prompter in the wings. In every Italian company the prompter plays a larger rôle than with us—a rôle Duse herself must remember, for, in the tale of her life, it is told how it was she who held the prompt book when she was 7 years old and her folks were on tour in Italy.

Such a prompter does not wait for a player's signal for help, but reads the script aloud in the wings, so that the actors can listen in whenever they need to.

At the Metropolitan, the hood of the box made him inaudible even to those of us who sat far forward. At the Century the sibilant clatter of him was a maddening accompaniment to the performance, though probably the Italians are as used to him as we are used to the honk of motor cars that penetrate to us from the city when we and the players may be astroll in Sherwood Forest. Or as we are grown used to the ructions of those playgoers who would not think of coming to the theater without their bronchitis.

Of course the name of Duse in the bills brought out all the people of the theater—attending in full force from May Irwin to Ben-Ami and Jane Cowl.

### III

Duse's third play was the gentle, simple peasant drama of mother love and heartache ineffable—the new piece called "Cosi Sia." We had never seen a great house full of playgoers sit so still, nor in recent years heard any play unfold in this town with so little of the incidental music of bronchitis. We had begun to believe that the old Bavarian king who had a theater built with only one seat in it was not so mad as his subjects like to believe. Now rises an heretical suspicion that coughing

in the audience bears some relation to what is afoot on
the stage, that bronchitis is a kind of dramatic criticism.
Certainly this audience followed breathlessly the performances of Duse and Memo Benassi and was not
heard from except in the cascades of applause which
followed each curtain.

It was difficult to watch this response without feeling
a regret that it had not been in "Cosi Sia" and at the
Century that Duse made her first reappearance in this
city. Here surely were none of the acres of people
smoldering, as at the Metropolitan, with a decent re-
sentment because they could not hear a word. Here
was a rôle which, for the most part, asks Duse to seem
just such a spent, fragile, white haired woman as she is.
And above all it was not only a good play but fortu-
nately an Italian one. Hearing that always dubious
and incorrigibly Norse drama "The Lady from the
Sea" being played in America by Italians had its crushing disadvantages—such disadvantages as might attend a French company's performance in Stockholm of
"La Première Année" by M. Frank Craven or "La
Veuve du Lycée" by le vieux George Ade.

Now, too, some progress had been made in tempering
the Century to Duse. Gone were those cold, cruel overhead lights which during the first performance of
"Ghosts" beat down on the devastation of her face and
underscored with black shadows the hollows of her
cheeks. Hushed almost to negligibility was the promp-

ter, who was now a mere faintly audible murmur—
seldom heard at all and never heard clearly.

Even with all these lightenings of her burden there
remains, of course, the irreconcilable division which ex-
ists now as it always existed. There are many play
goers of all levels of taste and discernment and sophis-
tication and background to whom she has nothing to say
—to whom she is just a wasted old woman moving
painfully through an alien play, eloquent of gesture,
perhaps, but at best a spirit of something that was.
There are others to whom she has a beauty and a truth
and an exaltation which arrest and stir them in ways
they had never found in the theater before. Your correspondent stands with these.

Duse is so commanding a figure that there is less
notice taken of an extraordinary actor of whom the
whole town would be talking had he come alone. That
is this Memo Benassi, who is heir apparent to the honors
that were Ando's when Duse played here long ago. He
has youth—they say he is no more than 26 years old—
he has vitality, fine dramatic fire and a voice for which
all the great rôles of the theater were written. They
say, too, that he is much sought in the motion picture
studios of France and Italy, but already nets are being
cast for him here and it should be no great surprise if
the news columns were to report some day that Benassi
would come back to us to take his chance with Ben-Ami
and young Schildkraut and the likes of them.

The Tuesday and Friday matinees at the Century
make possible a great attendance of American players.
One who called no roll at "Cosi Sia" and asked no
questions could, just from the vantage point of his own
seat see Louise Closser Hale, Laura Hope Crews, Grant
Mitchell, Frances Starr, Neil Martin, Grace Moore and
Florence Moore, all looking as though they had come
to church. D. W. Griffith was there too. He said
he had closed down his studio for the afternoon in
order that he might be on hand. He figured that
his seat to "Cosi Sia" cost him a little more than
$5,000.

There are sundry legends as to why, at the last
minute, the Norse "Lady from the Sea" was substituted
for the Italian "Cosi Sia" as the play for Duse's first performance in America. Our favorite among them points
out that the curtain rising on "Cosi Sia" would have
found her already on the stage, bent over a cradle and
hardly recognizable. The welcome then would have
come by fits and starts. But in "The Lady from the
Sea" she has what is known backstage as "an entrance." One likes to find so remote and lofty a
being as the legendary Duse caught when up to
the tricks of ordinary show folks. Such a discovery has in it something of the sense of humanity
which warms any sinner's heart when he catches a
priest in the human act of tucking away a nip of
Scotch.

## IV

Then came Praga's "La Porta Chiusa," chosen as the bill for the fourth week of Duse's engagement in New York. It is a modern Italian play about the hour in a woman's life when her son confronts her with his discovery that another than her husband had been his father.

This brief review is an account by one who went apprehensively, knowing how ragged some of the Duse productions can be, how uneven her own strength, how maddening the Italian prompter. Then "La Porta Chiusa" is the least of the plays in her repertory and its inclusion seemed a gesture of respect for young Benassi, who created the rôle of the son when the play was new in Milan some years ago. Nor was the apprehension dispelled when Duse herself came on. She looked like *Miss Havisham*, come blinking into the unaccustomed sunlight, so withered and so frail that she would not be able to meet even the little the play would ask her to do. Only once, in the ineffable wistfulness and sovereign beauty of her first good night, did she suggest the marvel that Duse can be and sometimes is.

Then came the second act, in which she sat on a little couch and told her tale. For those of us in whose inmost hearts she knows the chord, she was then a transformed being—vital, radiant, animate with a kind of truth that at once touches the earth and reaches to the stars, beautiful with the unclassifiable, unarguable beauty that is Eleonora Duse. When she said her next good night it was with a smile that filled the Century with a light not of this world.

The admirers of Benassi were a little disappointed. He has a magnificent equipment for the stage, but this time he was a trifle actory, with an excessive efflorescence of shrug and sob and gesture that smacked of brilliantine in the hair and recalled nothing so much as the somewhat trying performance Lowell Sherman gave on the first night of "Casanova." Then, for his big emotional scene, he squared off like a prima donna getting ready to assault an aria.

## V

Of the d'Annunzio plays which Duse bore from continent to continent twenty years ago only one is left in the repertory which she used in this belated return to us. That is "La Citta Morta," which was given as the first of her last two matinées in our town. It is a lush drama of the land of cypress and myrtle—the earthly torment of a blind saint, set forth with considerable theatric skill, the while d'Annunzio so luxuriates in the blue of the Ægean, the white of the dead city, the heavy incense of myrtle, the golden plash of fountains and the unbelieveable sweetness of lark music sung against a Greek sky that you are as suffocated by him as though you were spending the afternoon with one of those poets whose idea of life is to close all the windows and burn joss.

In the preface to the translation they sold in the lobby there was an almost intolerably intrusive and vulgar apology for giving a play by one who had hurt Duse so grievously. But for Duse herself it might be said that she feels sadly the shoddiness of her entire repertoire, and when she left Jolson's after her second visit to "The Brothers Karamazoff" she was more than a little ashamed that her own work was in plays less simple, less honest and less courageous than those of the Moscow Art Theater.

Of course, her cleansing voice is tonic to "La Citta Morta." It seemed on this afternoon that in no play on this visit had any rôle so suited her. Indeed, one wondered if the very wastage worked in the bitter score of years since last she played it here had not made her the more fit for its curious demands. Surely this blind prophetess should be embodied on the stage by one so little earthbound. The spell woven by her moving hands and by the moonlit magic of her voice wrought an ancient and mystic priestess for d'Annunzio's cluttered stage. For a little moment you thought that she whose ashes d'Annunzio wished to sift through the beautiful hands of another century had come to life again by invocation. And if it was not Cassandra, at least you knew this was no mere Italian actress now, but the noblest Roman of them all.

The Century was packed as usual, and, indeed, a
thwarted line of playgoers was coiled round the build-
ing like an angry snake. Certain burly fellows employed by the theater management for their interior
police had the time of their lives hurling out some im-
passioned compatriots of Duse's, who, with knives,
jimmies, crowbars and the like tried burgling their way
into the matinee.

## VI

Well, Duse has come and gone. Somehow this inde-
fatigable playgoer, in a month not altogether destitute
of other theatrical entertainment, managed to see eight
of her ten performances. After the last one the great
audience stayed on and on in the theater, seemingly
loath to say good-by. At that performance your correspondent gave up his own seats in order that John
Barrymore and Madge Kennedy might sit at Duse's
feet, and for the surrendered tickets he received a
premium rather richer than those demanded by the
regular scalpers along Broadway. It was the sight of
those two in tears at the rueful beauty and great tragic
truth of this Italian woman.

Whether Duse is now or ever was a good actress is, of
course, a matter of taste, and still more, a matter of
terms. Perhaps one might find the answer by speculating as to how well a whole company of Duses would
satisfy one's needs and desires in the theater. Cer-

tainly there is no clue in the mere fact that she has a
matchless beauty of speech and gesture, but probably
there is one in the fact that, in her, certain things of the
spirit find their clearest and their most persuasive voice.
Ancient and terrible fears, woe beyond words to tell,
find such a voice in the last despair of "La Citta
Morta." And among the things we shall remember to
the last of our days is the smile with which she says
good night to her son as the second act curtain falls in
"La Porta Chiusa." There she may not look and seem
the woman the playwright had in mind. In that moment, indeed, she is not an Italian mother saying good
night. Rather she is the thing itself. In that moment
she is mother love in benediction.

Yet the final gift she makes to some of us is something
else, something less easy to define and to acknowledge.
Most of us live in a scurrying and fretful world, jostled
and deafened by the hubbub of money grubbing, gossip,
foolish ambition and mean motive. We are the richer
who know in all the world one friend so withdrawn from it
in body or spirit that when we visit him it is like walking
among the far stars. On other footways than that of
the Grand Trunk Road of Hind, there still walk those
scattered brothers of the *Lama*, whose hand rested on the
wriggling shoulder of little *Kim*. And those of us whom
Duse moved most profoundly felt that here was another
who had seen the River of the Arrow and who was pausing to smile back at us from the Threshold of Freedom.

# MR. CHAPLIN

WHEN, after an absence of twenty years, Eleanora Duse returned to the New York stage, I saw her for the first time and saw, too, a kind of physical eloquence, a beauty of motion, which I had found only once before among the players of the world. That other one was Charles Chaplin, and if ever I have a motion picture machine in my cabin, it will be because I would like to look again from time to time at such pictures as "Shoulder Arms," "The Kid" and "The Pilgrim," just as I would keep "Huckleberry Finn" always on my shelf and, if I could afford it, a Renoir or a Forain always on my wall.

If, as sometimes happens, a neighbor tells me that this or that zany of the screen or stage is much, much funnier than Chaplin, I am at a loss for words because, after all, it is not merely or chiefly as a comic that he is great. One who seldom uses the word "great" would not hesitate to use it here. After all Chaplin does not rattle around even in the word "genius."

It is one of the customs of the parvenus among the *intelligentsia* to extol the art of Mr. Chaplin in one breath and to use the next for the purpose of deploring the boisterous comicalities in which he indulges. It is true enough that "The Pilgrim" is a little less aspiring in its content than some of its predecessors. But to my notion it is rich in the kind of homely, sturdy humor with which Mark Twain enlivened his epic of the Mississippi. And anyway Chaplin himself, always a universal figure like Jack Frost or Robin Goodfellow, imparts to any tale he tells something of the glamor and flavor of an old nursery legend, a tale told for a thousand years around a thousand drowsy hearths.

Not that "The Pilgrim" is not independently good. Indeed, Chaplin himself is so amazing an instrument— there are soaring moments in this picture when the winged Chaplin of Hollywood embodies the poetry of motion as surely and as fully as does the Winged Victory of Samothrace—he himself is so sensitive, so delicate and so exquisitely graduated a player that one is apt to overlook the warm humanity and the crafty inventiveness that are in the episodes which make up his pictures. Such inventiveness, for instance, as is shown in the notion that the escaped convict would, in buying his railroad ticket, have to struggle to keep his hands from straying absent-mindedly to the iron bars in front of the ticket window. Or in the notion that this little vagrant, mistaken for the new minister because he had fled in the garb of a natatorial clergyman, would think, after preaching in pantomime a magnificent ser-

mon on David and Goliath, that he ought to rush back
into the pulpit and take a bow, take one of those circus
calls, head on one side and arms outstretched in so perfect a *tya-da* gesture that you can almost hear the blare
of the trumpets. Or the notion that during the collection he would be alternately suspicious of the plate
passers and worried for fear they would overlook that
fat man over in the corner of the pew who had not given
a cent yet. And that he would finally become so excited that his hand would stray abstractedly to his
pocket and a Camel would be half way to his lips before
he knew it.

In his scene with one exasperating little brat in "The
Pilgrim" Chaplin does the kind of thing which sets up
a crossroads at which his critics part company. To my
notion it is an immensely and deeply satisfying scene,
because in it Chaplin does what we all want to do, but,
being oppressed by civilization, do not do. At a tea,
one garrulous mother's soiled, restless and inventive
child strays over to the sofa, where the uneasy Chaplin
sits primly. The child tugs at his coat, punches him
tentatively in the ribs and then climbs up the more
easily to thrust a grimy finger in his eye. Then he emp-
ties part of the contents of the goldfish bowl down the
sufferer's neck. But the sufferer is at a tea and tradition bids him smile and smile and be a gentleman. So,
with a frozen leer which only the careless could mistake for amiability, he keeps putting the little dear

from him, patting the darling's head with a gingerly hand and bidding him go play with mamma. Comes a moment when the grown-ups leave the room. The child, left alone with Chaplin, renews his assaults. And Chaplin, with a great calm enveloping his soul, with a gesture admirable in its reticence, with, indeed, an expression of simple earnestness, kicks the child in the stomach. This exploit is, I believe, the kind of thing the defectives have in mind when they say Chaplin is vulgar. They are unconsciously right to the extent—and only to the extent—that the language he speaks is the vulgate of everyday emotions.

But the high point in "The Pilgrim" is reached in the final episode. The big battle scarred sheriff has recognized the fugitive as the fellow pictured in the placards offering a reward for his return to jail. The sheriff has grown to like the little cuss, and there are lines of searing reluctance in the official face as he rides off toward the railroad station dragging his prey by the collar. The welling sympathy in the official heart overflows when he passes the borderland crossroads, where the United States ends and Mexico begins. The sheriff looks the other way to give the little rascal a chance, and is visibly disappointed when he looks back again and finds his captive waiting patiently for further instructions. The sheriff's roving eye lights on a tuft of flowers growing on a hillock far beyond the border. He bids Chaplin go pick them for him. For a moment

the incredulous prisoner stares in astonishment at the
red, sweaty, hairy face thus demanding a nosegay.
Then he scurries across the line and is lost to sight.
Over the face aforesaid there spreads a smile that is
half benevolence, half amused content. And it is still
there as the sheriff turns his horse's head toward home,
gives a shake to the reins and jogs away. The picture
seems about to fade into nothingness, when suddenly,
over the edge of the landscape, comes to a cloud of dust.
And out of it, tearing along for dear life, a pure and innocent heart pumping overtime, a world of conscientious-
ness expressed in the very line of the ducked head and
in every wiggle of those traveling legs, comes Chaplin—
bringing the flowers. It was almost more than I could
bear.

This enthusiasm for the matchless art of Charlie
Chaplin is not new in my repertoire of enthusiasms.
I hope that no one will misread these paragraphs as the
output of one who is just taking him up in a serious
way. It is astounding how every season some one does
do that. No year ever has a chance to slip by without
some self-important fellow getting to his feet and announcing his own discovery that this Chaplin fellow is
no mere buffoon, but a comedian of considerable
ability. One could endure the belatedness of these
handsome recognitions if they were not always couched
in the intolerably condescending language of some one
who has been slumming among the amusements of the

multitude. Not long ago a luncheon was rendered un-palatable for me when a hack writer of no little popular reputation rose and spoke thus benignly and graciously of one whose shoelaces, artistically, he was not fit to tie.

There was a time, however, when there was some point to such cheer leading for Chaplin, when his stand-ing as an artist had not been canonized. The way, I think, was led by one of our true wise men—Harvey O'Higgins. And it was in those days that Mrs. Fiske did something unusual for her. She sat down and wrote a magazine article. For *Harper's Weekly*, in the days when its torch had fallen from the hands of George Harvey into the hands of Norman Hapgood, Mrs. Fiske wrote a piece about Chaplin which was a gesture of obeisance. She put her finger on his secret—"the old, familiar secret of an inexhaustible imagination governed by the unfailing precision of a perfect tech-nique. To the writer," Mrs. Fiske went on, "Charles Chaplin appears as a great comic artist, possessing in-spirational powers and a technique as unfailing as Réjane's. If it be treason to Art to say this, then let those exalted persons who allow culture to be defined only on their own terms make the most of it."

# COPEY

THE card tables were banished one wintry night from the long, chaste room on the second floor of the Harvard Club, and every inch of its space was taken up by a miscellany of young and middle aged graduates who had one thing in common. They had all studied under Copeland. And this year, as once every year since 1906, when the custom was started, he had come down from Cambridge to read to them. It is an annual observance of an old, deeply felt friendship, and probably there is no reunion quite like it anywhere in America. This report is made by a barbarian who had smuggled his way into that Attic gathering, a Hamilton man who did not belong there at all and yet wished much to attend, however belatedly, a class held by one who, in an innocent, indirect and hazily remote way, had been responsible for his going to college at all.

The story begins in Philadelphia more than twenty years ago. It was a time when folks were wondering idly whether Cyrus Curtis and his new editor, George Horace Lorimer, would ever succeed in their fantastic project of turning Benjamin Franklin's old weekly into a prosperous national magazine. Among the first serials, followed eagerly from week to week at our house, were the "Calumet K." story, which Sam Merwin and Henry Kitchell Webster wrote together, and the letters from the self-made merchant which Lorimer himself was writing. And along about that time this new *Saturday Evening Post* published a story called "The Diary of a Freshman," by Charles Macomb Flandrau, still the best tale of its kind that has passed my way and, by allaying the misgivings to which Captain King's alarming "Cadet Days" had given birth, definitely the influence which implanted in me the idea that it would be a pleasant and an adventurous thing to go to college.

All my subsequently verified or corrected notions of undergraduate life were derived from that Flandrau story, and in it the most interesting and most persuasive figure was an abstracted and whimsical instructor named *Fleetwood*. One young reader's friendship with *Fleetwood* began from the moment he wandered into the story, vaguely shooing *Granny Wood* out of a certain chair at a restaurant and sinking into it with the murmured apology: "I'm an old man, but I know my place." It deepened when he invited the freshman to one of his Wednesday evenings, and on being asked when they were held answered sadly and a little shamefacedly, "On Wednesday evenings." As the story progressed *Fleetwood*, provocative, charming, amusing and more than a little intimidating, emerged in gradual significance as an idea of what a teacher might be.

It happened that a curious accident deflected me, thank God, from Harvard. To be sure, there was no one quite like *Fleetwood* at Hamilton, but, of course, no one who studied under Square Root and knew him in the booklined study of his eighteenth century house across the road from the Hamilton campus would ever accept any one in his place as an exchange professor.

It must have been a good many years later that *Fleetwood* was identified for me as the man who is known in the register of Harvard University as Prof. Charles Townsend Copeland, and known to all the latter day Harvard men as Copey. Around that name sundry legends have accumulated, tales told of him by such warm admirers of his as Mrs. Fiske, say, or John D. Williams, or Edward Sheldon, or John Barrymore. Going out to tea at Prof. Copeland's rooms in Hollis Hall is one of the rites that Mrs. Fiske counts on when some new play takes her down Boston way. Once she was bent on such a pilgrimage when she was waylaid on her arrival in Cambridge by some of the students, among them, perhaps, the same young Sheldon who was soon to write the "Salvation Nell" in which she played so magically. They bore her off to some such place as the *Advocate* office, and she was being vastly entertained when a messenger arrived with a note which produced a great flutter, and away she went in a

flurry of farewells and contrition.  The note had said:
"Minnie, come over to Copey's."

Barrymore loves to tell of a night whiled away when
he was playing in Boston, a night of delightful conversation with Prof. Copeland, which the actor prolonged
indefinitely by the simple expedient of waiting each
time until the professor would be getting into his coat
and hat and then dropping casually some observation
about life or art or letters so hopelessly ignorant that
Copey would just have to sit down and argue about it.

Several of the younger fry among the critics in our
town are Copeland students, among them Kenneth
Macgowan, Heywood Broun, Robert C. Benchley and
Gilbert Seldes.  Mr. Broun was always afraid of him
and to this day at sight of him shifts uneasily from foot
to foot like an elephant with something on its mind.
Once when he was reporting some game at Harvard, he
was due to catch a New York train immediately afterward and deliver his copy in New York. So he paid his
visit to 15 Hollis in the morning, knowing he would not
have a minute to spare after the game.  He plodded up
the stairs to the fine, old, quite assertively Eighteenth
Century room under the roof, stuck his head in the door
and was greeted by the spectacle of the professor deep
in converse with some student.  Copeland waved him
out: "Go way, Heywood.  Come back at 5:30 this
afternoon."  "Yes, sir," said Mr. Broun from force of
habit, and was half way down the stairs before he

realized it meant he would have to telegraph his copy and remain overnight in Boston. The story was telegraphed.

Among the most active members of the Charles Townsend Copeland Association is Maxwell Perkins of *Scribner's*. Like many another editor or publisher, he has long had his hopes pinned on a volume of Copeland's reminiscences, and once, they say, even extracted a promise that they would be begun at once and diligently written until the final chapter would be ready for the printers. It is gravely to be doubted whether so much as a paragraph is yet on paper. Once Perkins telegraphed from New York that he would be leaving by the next train to collect the first installment. An answering wire intimated that the reminiscence would not be started for quite some time. "Come up eight years from now," was the wording of the discouragement.

At his class on the night I attended, after the room had been properly aired, the drafts adjusted and all the cigars and cigarettes yielded up as a sort of half burnt sacrifice on the altar of this friendship, the teacher came walking down the aisle, with all of us standing and applauding and beaming. The readings included "Little Flower of the Wood," one of the trickiest tales in Merrick's "A Chair on the Boulevard"; also Kipling's "Mandalay" and "The Truce of the Bear," together with the sage outgivings of Mr. Dooley on the subject of this latter poem, which was sung in the days when "the czars in Russia called themselves czars." Then there was Thackeray's "Ballade of Bouillabaisse," and to the accompaniment of great hilarity certain irreverent passages from the most comical book of the winter, "Perfect Behavior," by Donald Ogden Stewart. Altogether it was a flagrantly popular program, one nicely calculated to delight its audience and to pain unspeakably any professor who had taken his Ph.D. by writing a thesis on the use of the indefinite article in Edmund Spenser. Prof. Copeland is an artful reader with a superb dramatic voice, but the thing in his reading which warms it and spreads that warmth throughout the room is his own great relish of the beauty and the fun and humanity in the books into which he dips.

He was then in his sixty-third year. In his parting word that night there was the implicit promise of many another such evening in the years ahead. His ambition, he said, was to walk in the ways of Manuel Garcia, who was a teacher until his hundredth year and then turned into a cigar.

## MALBROUGH S'EN VA-T-EN GUERRE

AMONG the good things that Balieff gave us in the second year of his American visit was a song they have been singing in France for more than two centuries, but which, as far as we can recall, had not been sung in our town in our time. That is the half jaunty, half pensive ballad called *Le Mort et Convoi de l'Invincible Malbrough*. Every Frenchman knows it—knows it so thoroughly that he could not for the life of him tell when and where it first entered into his memories any more than any of us can remember at what time and place we first heard "Yankee Doodle."

There are those who say its tune runs back to the time of the Crusades—that the knights of Godfrey de Bouillon roared it under the very walls of Jerusalem, leaving it behind them in Arabia, where you can hear it to this day. Certainly its association with the mock ballad of the dread Duke of Marlborough goes back to the Battle of Malplaquet, in 1709, at a time when his was a name wherewith the *bonnes* could frighten children into good behavior. Unable to slay or rout the fellow, it was the French way to take revenge in derisive song, and the legend has it that at nightfall

65

after the disastrous battle a French soldier, who was minus his shirt by this time and had not eaten in three days, distilled for himself a sweet consolation by inditing this funeral dirge for an enemy then only too painfully alive.

The song spread along the line from tent to tent and became one of the homely and cheerful possessions of the people. Years later—later by three score years and ten—it was taken to court. A son had been born to the alien Queen, and to Versailles was summoned a ruddy, buxom peasant woman to be his nurse. With her from the country she brought the old tune which, as like as not, her grandfather had heard sung along the road in the confusion after Malplaquet. So the cradle of the little chap, who was to vanish into history as the Lost Dauphin, was rocked to the incongruous melody of *Malbrough s'en va-t-en guerre.*

It caught the ear and jingled in the memory of the Austrian, to whom it was a new thing in a land where so much was still new. She made it the fad of Versailles. It was played by the fiddlers of the court. It was hummed and roared in the stables. It spread to Paris and became the rage. Its lugubrious tale was wrought in tapestries and embroideries. It was painted on fans and carved on snuff boxes. The *Mironton, mironton, mirontaine* dogged the stranger's steps along the Seine much as the *What, never? Well, hardly ever* refrain became epidemic in this country when "Pinafore" was new. The song maddened the young Goethe, agape in the Paris of Louis XVI. It was a favorite with Napoleon, who, though no great shakes as a barytone, made a point of singing its catch lines as he put foot to stirrup for any entry into battle.

Up on our own Century Roof its elegiac quatrians were acted out with mock solemnity by a very troupe of puppets escaped from some lunatic Guignol. The sound of the accompanying verses stirred many a memory in this listening chronicler. A memory of an old woman in a smoky, sausage-festooned kitchen of a Norman *estaminet*, bending over the fire and beating an omelette to the rhythm of *Mironton, mironton, mirontaine*. A memory of three little *poilus* in weather stained *horizon bleu*, jogging under a wintry moon along the white, frosted road that led to Nancy and singing as they went *Malbrough s'en va-t-en guerre*. A memory of a dirt-floor farmhouse on the Brittany coast—a lonely farmhouse built when the great Louis was King of France. And there one summer night while the crowd sat around the wall to listen and someone with a guitar strummed a lazy accompaniment, our own Kathleen Howard stood and sang this ancient song.

Above all, a memory of "Trilby." Occasional references to that book of books will keep creeping into these pages as King Charles's head into Mr. Dick's memorial. Every reasonable effort will be made to avoid them, but surely this time it is necessary. For that night when

*Taffy* and the *Laird* and *Little Billee* went to the *Cirque des Bashibazoucks* to hear *La Svengali* sing—the night they learned that it was *Trilby*—the greatest voice of all time imparted its immeasurable heartache to this foolish old ballad. It is a matchless description, that passage wherein Du Maurier follows verse by verse the mounting anxiety, the deepening sense of an irrevocable calamity with which she could invest the coming of the messenger. Hear him:

"All this time the accompaniment had been quite simple—just a few obvious, ordinary chords.

"But now, quite suddenly, without a single modulation or note of warning, down goes the tune a full major third, from E to C—into the graver depths of *Trilby's* great contralto—so solemn and ominous that there is no more weeping, but the flesh creeps; the accompaniment slows and elaborates itself; the march becomes a funeral march, with muted strings and quite slowly:

> Aux nouvelles que j'apporte—
> *Mironton, mironton, mirontaine!*
> Aux nouvelles que j'apporte,
> Vos beaux yeux vont pleurer!

"Richer and richer grows the accompaniment. The *mironton, mirontaine* becomes a dirge:

> Quittez vos habits roses—
> *Mironton, mironton, mirontaine!*
> Quittez vos habits roses,
> Et vos satins brochés?

"Here the ding-donging of a big bell seems to mingle with the score . . . and very slowly, and so impressively that the news will ring forever in the ears and hearts of those who hear it from *La Svengali's* lips:

> Le Sieur Malbrouck est mort—
>   *Mironton, mironton, mirontaine!*
> Le Sieur—Malbrouck—est—mort!
>   Est mort—et enterré!

"And thus it all ends quite abruptly.

"And this heartrending tragedy, this great historical epic in two dozen lines at which some five or six thousand gay French people are sniffing and mopping their eyes like so many Niobes, is just a common old French comic—a mere nursery ditty like 'Little Bopeep.'"

But the full ballad as it has been handed down through the generations is much longer than two dozen lines and here, for once in a way, is the whole thing:

## LE MORT ET CONVOI DE L'INVINCIBLE MALBROUGH

> Malbrough s'en va-t-en guerre.
> Mironton, mironton, mirontaine.
> Malbrough s'en va-t-en guerre,
> Ne sait quand reviendra.
>
> Il reviendra z-a Pâques,
> Mironton, mironton, mirontaine,
> Il reviendra z-a Pâques,
> Ou à la Trinité.

La Trinité se passe
Mironton, mironton, mirontaine,
La Trinité se passe
Malbrough ne revient pas

Madame a sa tour monté,
Mironton, mironton, mirontaine.
Madame a sa tour monté
Si haut qu'elle peut monter.

Elle aperçoit son pag'e
Mironton, mironton, mirontane.
Elle aperçoit son pag'e
Tout de noir habillé.

Beau pag'e, ah! mon beau pag'e.
Mironton, mironton, mirontaine.
Beau pag'e, ah! mon beau pag'e
Quell' nouvelle apportez.

Aux nouvell's que j'apporte,
Mironton, mironton, mirontaine.
Aux nouvell's que j'apporte,
Vos beaux yeux vont pleurer.

Quittez vos habits roses,
Mironton, mironton, mirontaine,
Quittez vos habits roses
Et vos satins brochés.

Monsieur d'Malbrough est mort.
Mironton, mironton, mirontaine,
Monsieur d'Malbrough est mort.
Est mort et enterré.

J'lai vu porter en terre.
Mironton, mironton, mirontane.
J'lai vu porter en terre,
Par quatre z-officiers.

L'un portait sa cuirasse.
Mironton, mironton, mirontaine.
L'un portait sa cuirasse,
L'autre son boucler.

L'un portait son grand sabre.
Mironton, mironton, mirontaine,
L'un portait son grand sabre,
L'autre ne portait rien.

A l'entour de sa tombe.
Mironton, mironton, mirontaine,
A l'entour de sa tombe,
Romarins, l'on planta.

Sur la plus haute branche.
Mironton, mironton, mirontaine,
Sur la plus haute branche,
Le rossig'nol chanta.

On vit voler son ame,
Mironton, mironton, mirontaine.
On vit voler son ame.
Au travers des lauriers.

Chacun mit ventre à terre
Mironton, mironton, mirontaine.
Chacun mit ventre à terre.
Et puis se releva.

Pour chanter les victoires,
Mironton, mironton, mirontaine,
Pour chanter les victoires
Que Malbrough remporta.

La ceremonie faite,
Mironton, mironton, mirontaine.
La ceremonie faite.
Chacun s'en fut coucher.

Les uns avec leurs femmes.
Mironton, mironton, mirontaine.
Les uns avec leurs femmes,
Et les autres tout seuls.

Ce n'est pas qu'il en manque.
Mironton, mironton, mirontaine.
Ce n'est pas qu'il en manque
Car j'en connais beaucoup.

Des blondes et des brunes.
Mironton, mironton, mirontaine.
Des blondes et des brunes
Et des chataign's aussi.

J'n'en dis pas davantage.
Mironton, mironton, mirontaine.
J'n'en dis pas davantage,
Car en voilà z-assez.

From this version is carefully omitted the sinful
final quatrain especially written for the Russian zanies
on the Century Roof. In his ambling preamble to the
ballad there, Balieff had the hardihood to repeat the old
tale about the days when this song was so all-pursuing

in Europe. It seems a Frenchman astray in London and bound for Marlborough street could not remember its name, but got there all right by hailing a cab and enriching the cabby's day by singing "*Malbrough*" to him. Balieff also proudly claims for this ballad the distinction of never having been turned into what he balefully calls a fawx trawt. Perhaps so, perhaps not. But the tune did cross over to England and thence to us nearly a hundred years ago. And we hear it every year of our lives, for the words that it picked up in England were "We won't go home until morning."

Anyway, it was altogether delightful to hear it sung so solemnly, so nonsensically in the Chauve-Souris. And perhaps, if we are all very good, some day Balieff may bring over another French song that has hidden too long in old French buvettes and garrisons—"*Aupres de ma blonde.*"

# "THE SIX BEST PLAYS"

INCITED by the dramatic editor of *The Sun and The Globe*, your humble servant once raked his memory to determine what were the six plays he had most enjoyed in all his days as a theatergoer. The question was put to a wide variety of connoisseurs, ranging all the way from Secretary of Labor Davis to Gilda Gray. The answers came in from playgoers who could remember the productions which Phelps made at Sadler's Wells and from others who appeared to have become theatergoers so recently that they were not quite ready yet with a list of six.

This symposium was only part of a current passion for list making—a passion so hot and so general that there have already been evidences of reaction. Thus while Franklin P. Adams has indulged himself in agreeable speculation as to the identity of the ten women with whom he would most enjoy being shipwrecked on a desert island, *Vanity Fair* has gravely submitted several lists of the Ten Dullest Authors.

Even in that playful compilation there were signs of humbug. For instance, while it is altogether plausible that Edna Ferber never knew any book to yield her

so little entertainment as did her "Plane Geometry,"
it seems at least doubtful if Carl Van Vechten and
Ernest Boyd really regard Barrie as one of the world's
ten dullest authors. They were just showing off.

Such humbug invariably attends these symposiums,
and, being apparent or suspected, dilutes their interest.
The man who in all his days since the First Reader
never enjoyed any book so much as "The Prisoner of
Zenda" will faithlessly strike it out of his list in favor
of Voltaire's "Candide," in the hope of impressing onlookers as cultured, profound, or at the least, odd.
But the chief trouble encountered in making out such
a list lies, not in the temptation to pose and strut. It
lies in the real difficulty of being exact. This is set
down here as the experience of one who, with much
rumination and anxious precision had no sooner finished
his own list for *The Sun and The Globe* than he knew
full well that the six plays he named were not the six he
had most enjoyed.

What were the six plays I enjoyed most? Probably
the best answer would have been "Aw, shucks, I can't
remember." But lacking the gumption, the taci-
turnity and the informality to make that response, I
set to pondering. Obviously it would not do merely to
name the six best plays I had ever seen, for while such
a list would have to include "Candida," for instance,
and "Hedda Gabler," it so happens that I enjoyed
neither of them greatly when I saw them. It so hap-

pens that I have never seen either of them decently acted. The only tolerable *Candida* I ever saw had an elderly, weatherbeaten and ear splitting *Marchbanks* rending the air in her vicinity. Of the two stray *Heddas* that have been my lot, one was frowsy, middle aged and unappetizing—the other was mountainous, majestical and inarticulate in the language spoken. Some day some one will have sense enough to put on "Hedda Gabler" with either Emily Stevens, Christine Norman or Lynn Fontanne as *Hedda*, whereupon I shall be glad to lead the dancing in the streets. Until Ethel Barrymore plays *Candida* I never expect fully to enjoy that play—or Ethel Barrymore.

You may enjoy a play for such varied and impermanent reasons. A dull farce may become iridescent if you have been lucky enough to have had Chateauneuf du Pape with your dinner or to have persuaded the loveliest person in the world to overcome her explicable reluctance about being seen with you at the theater. Indeed it would be simple enough for me to draw up a list of the six plays I had really enjoyed most if only I were permitted to explain at length why I had enjoyed them. Such a list, with footnotes, would include the following not especially notable theatrical performances:

"The Arabian Nights," by Sydney Grundy.

A certain animal act playing the Shubert Vaudeville Theater in Utica in 1908.

The Royal Lilliputians at the Coates Opera House, Kansas City, Mo.

"The Survival of the Fittest."

These four were enjoyed at the time for widely different reasons. Consider, for instance, the case of the Royal Lilliputians. The details of the performance have drifted out of memory, but vivid still is the glamour that surrounded it—a glamour never since recaptured in the theater. That confession can be made freely enough by one who, even in his comparative senescence, has been known to become not unenthusiastic at the play. I saw the Royal Lilliputians when I was 4 years old. It was my first trip to the theater. The occasion subjected me thus early to a habit which has since become ineradicable, for I went on press seats that had been sent to the Kansas City *Star* and from the office of that excellent journal had been purloined for our use by Roswell Field, Eugene Field's brother, who was the first column conductor of them all.

Or consider "The Survival of the Fittest," a drama by a man named Atkinson, which was seen briefly at the Greenwich Village Theater some seasons ago. It has had its close seconds, before and since, but it seems to me, after considerable reflection, to have been the worst show I ever saw. It is not an uncommon experience for the first nighters to encounter plays so terrible that no subsequent audience is ever subjected to them.

On such occasions, a weak mannerliness, combined with sympathy for the players, bids us all betray no other emotion than a certain embarrassment and perhaps a disposition to slip away into the night. But "The Survival of the Fittest" was so wildly atrocious that one felt free to cry out and roll in the aisle. Clear as crystal even now are the two high moments. One was when Laura Nelson Hall, as a somewhat too vigorous helpmeet, leaped heartlessly over the dying body of her husband (George Le Guerre) and went out into the garden for amorous converse with her lover (Montague Love), whence their hearty laughter floated in as an accompaniment to the ensuing death scene. The other was that moment when Winfred Lenihan made a gift to her father's burly gardener (Mr. Love), with whom, oddly enough, she was dancing. Out of the bosom of her gown she shyly drew a safety razor, all put together ready for use, but he scornfully tossed it aside as a toy too frail for his beard. The performance by Mr. Love elicited from Heywood Broun in the *Tribune* one of the most telling descriptions of acting published in our time. "Mr. Love's idea of playing a he man," said Mr. Broun, "was to extend his chest three inches and then follow it slowly across the stage." All in all, I never enjoyed any play more than "The Survival of the Fittest." No one who saw it will ever forget it.

The animal act referred to was enjoyable because of an episode in the performance not forecast in the program.

It was not, as recalled now after fifteen years, an especially brilliant zoo transplanted to the stage of the Shubert. It was just a collection of underfed little monkeys who reluctantly performed certain tricks at the somewhat urgent request of a stout lady in black silk doublet and hose who had to maintain discipline among them, and in the stormier heart of a baboon chained to the center of the stage. She maintained it by the canny device of withholding their supper until after the performance. Presumably the wayward were not fed at all. On this particular day, as one of the undergraduates from Hamilton who invariably occupied the front row at the Shubert, I had all unwittingly brought in some refreshments of my own from the sidewalk. The act was in full swing when, quite without sinister purpose, I cracked a peanut. At that lovely sound, every member of the troupe halted, looked about him with a wild surmise and then raced to the footlights and peered eagerly into the darkness of the auditorium. The stout lady brandished her whip and spoke to them unkindly. They waved her aside with their tails. Not realizing what it was all about, I watched, fascinated, and in my abstraction cracked another peanut. It was too much. With whimperings of excitement and hope the monkeys flung themselves across the orchestra pit and into our arms—all of them except the unhappy baboon, who fell over the footlights and was rapidly being hanged to death when rescued timidly

by the second trombone.    Down came the curtain,
the displeasure of the lady in tights could be heard
through its folds, and the ushers skated down the
aisles to notify us all that we would have to leave.
What the rest of the bill was like I never knew, but up
to that point it had been the most enjoyable I had ever
known.

The delightful performance of "The Arabian Nights"
that I have in mind was one given at the Scollard
Opera House, Clinton, N. Y., sometime in 1908.    That
theater is a not notably modern or beautiful temple
of the drama which belongs (though you would never
think it to look at it) to Clinton Scollard.    It was built
upstairs long before Master Ziegfeld and his lamented
(by some) frolic were ever heard of.    As a matter of fact,
it is over the grocery store.    The company which, at
the time, seemed so extraordinary in "The Arabian
Nights," thereafter retired from the stage.    The
ingenue has since put in his time as poison expert for
the United States Army, and the *jeune premier* led a
machine gun detachment on the Somme.    One comedian
has built up a nationally known advertising business, and
another is a professor of literature.    The Irish maid in
that farce has just returned from walking 2,000 miles
through the Congo jungle in quest of gold.    The indi-
vidual performance which I enjoyed most, however,
and which every one agreed was superb, was given by

a not widely known player who has since become a dramatic critic in New York.

But to have named "The Arabian Nights" or any of these personal favorites would have been to run the dread danger of being misunderstood. So refuge was taken in rephrasing the question to make it read: "Of the plays you have enjoyed in the theater, name the six you would most like to see again next week if you could see them as well played." And the six which seemed best to meet that test were "The Gods of the Mountain" (as it was given by The Amateur Comedy Club of New York), "The Man Who Married a Dumb Wife" (produced by Barker), "The Old Lady Shows Her Medals," "A Kiss for Cinderella," "Le Paquebot Tenacity" (as Copeau first staged it in Paris) and the Ames revival of "Pierrot the Prodigal."

# PAULINE LORD

THE tale the cables told of something that happened in London one night in the Spring of 1922, released suddenly from its cubby hole in the memory an experience that had been mine in the now half incredible days of 1918 when the German empire was gathering its huge forces to strike a last blow at Paris. It was at the time when the sultry lull that followed the bloody work in the Bois de Belleau was interrupted by the unwonted spectacle of several platoons of the Marines and the Ninth and Twenty-third Infantry being pulled out of the line, deloused, shaved and bathed. The excitement was tremendous. Word spread rapidly that they were being beautified for the Fourth of July parade of the Allies in Paris. This explanation at first was received with skepticism, for these troops and the wilder boys of the Rainbow were always laboring under the delusion that they were about to be sent somewhere to parade. Why, even on that desperate night of rain a fortnight later when Foch seized them all like a javelin and hurled them through the drenched forest of Villers Cotteret, the night when their crowded trucks hustled

them without food or water along the black roads that
led to Soissons, their innocent hearts were sustained by
a secret conviction that they were being rushed to a
port so that they could return to New York and be
exhibited there as an advertisement of the A. E. F.
And high time, too.

But on this occasion earlier in July the rumor happened to be right. And when this became apparent
all of their camp followers started hooking rides on the
ambulances that streaked down through La Ferté and
Meaux to Paris.

The morning of that anxious Fourth was overcast
and a feathery mist hung above the Seine. But the
holiday crowds in the Place de la Concorde and the
Champs Elysées were enormous. And because the memory of Belleau Wood was fresh and the news was out
that the Americans at last were landing in numbers
sufficient to amount to something, there was a great
craning of French necks to see how they would be repre-
sented in the parade.

Your correspondent stood on a trembling chair and
watched the celebration across acres of bobbing heads.
First came the little poilus, scuffling along unpre-
tentiously in their streaked and faded horizon bleu.
Then there were the French cavalrymen, spirited and
spectacular with their brandished swords. Then the
Americans—the Sammies, as the French newspapers
still revoltingly described them. As the first of them

trooped by, there was no more than the hubbub of ordinary good will, for they were so obviously just the neat noncombatants that had littered up Paris all year, clerks in the insurance office, M. P.'s from Gen. Hart's dungeon keeps, medical department orderlies with the brassards on their arms, all a little white and soft when compared with the battered French soldiers who had preceded them.

Then suddenly from far up the avenue came the sound of something different—a rumble of cheering that swelled till it was like a roar of oncoming waters. For a while it was impossible to see what was causing it, but the excitement was near, nearer. Then it engulfed us, for there under the shower of blossoms tossed down from the French planes that were swooping and circling just overhead, stepping along with magnificent unconcern, were the doughboys of the Second Division. They were the men from Château-Thierry and the crowds knew them by their helmets and their faces and the look and air of them.

It was a much uplifted onlooker who felt himself choking and who might have disgraced himself by an outbreak of which the nation could never have approved had he not been overpowered at the moment by the deeper emotion of embarrassment. For just then a bevy of old French women with their grandchildren, frustrated in their fond efforts to get through the crowd and at the marchers, contented themselves by pelting him, instead, with roses. What he lacked as an approximation to their ideals of American soldiery he made up, perhaps, in his excellence as a target. Anyway, he knew that every Frenchman in that tossing multitude was thinking: "Here is the real thing from America at last," and he was glowing with pride because those men who, in the strange whirligig of history, were filing along the Avenue of the Elysian Fields that morning were his own countrymen.

All of which may seem a journey around Robin Hood's barn to reach the Star Theater in London, where "Anna Christie" was presented with the same company that had acted the play when it was given in New York for twenty-seven weeks at the Vanderbilt. And if it had been my portion to be in the stalls that night watching the same audience which had politely experienced so many premières of third rate American plays with second rate American players should have felt the same emotion which strangled me that July morning in Paris five years before. There certainly was the real thing from America at last. The cheering was so great it could be heard in New York.

Even though it turned out that the London playgoer, used to the dramatic dishwater that had been his fare for so many seasons, proved unable to digest such strong and bitter meat as "Anna Christie" for longer than a brief diet, nothing could disturb our first contentment. London had now seen Pauline Lord in an

O'Neill play, and so for the first time in this generation knew what the young American theater could do. The cabled excerpts from the newspaper reviews had all the recognition for the strength of this play and the magnificence of this actress that their friends at home could possibly have asked.

We read in the *Morning Post*, which described O'Neill as one of the greatest English speaking dramatists who, "alone, or almost alone, has big ideas," this further shrewd comment on him: "His men and women express themselves vividly enough in their talk, but when the time for action comes their characters do not give way or lose their shape under the strain, as do the flimsy creatures of most playwrights. And so, though you may not like the story he tells, you never doubt it." The *Daily News* said: "Seldom has such cheering been heard in the theater. It may hurt the pride of our own actresses, but we know of none fitted by age for the part of *Anna Christie* who could act with such subtlety, surety and emotional effect." And it was good to find Walkley in the *Times* saying: "When the chance was hers, Miss Lord took it with amazing delicacy and power. Her performance cast over the theater a spell now very rare, for it held beyond the emotion it immediately created and when the tempest was past, subtleties appeared in the memory which in the instant had not been consciously perceived."

Probably the satisfaction which all this recognition

began in those watching from home had some of its origin in a knowledge of what a long, hard pull the theater had meant for Pauline Lord. When the battered leading woman of the Milwaukee stock company has the kind of great night in London of which the hungry newcomers who play the parlor maids dream at night in their cheerless hall bedrooms, the onlooker feels the glow of a happy ending and a renewed suspicion that there may be some justice in the world after all. Admittedly my own glow was greater because O'Neill and Pauline Lord were Americans doing us all proud in an alien hand. And if that be patriotism, make the most of it.

# THE PARIS TAXI-DRIVER CONSIDERED AS AN ARTIST

It was not so very long ago that E. V. Lucas, one of the most affectionate and understanding of all the latter-day pilgrims to the city of cities, dwelling fondly on the gay old *cochers* who used to add such color, zest, and even hazard to travel in the streets of Paris, dismissed as a negligibly remote nightmare the day when automobiles would, to any considerable extent, replace the carriages. There were, he admitted, such distant objectives as Barbizon, say, or Sannois, for which motor traffic would be convenient. But, though other cities might rank convenience above charm, in Paris, at least, there would always survive those languid victorias which the English novelists like to call *fiacres* and which the perverse Parisians persist in calling *sapins*. (Though how a word of such funereal connotation ever became attached, behind the Academy's back, to so festive a vehicle passes all comprehension.)

Regretfully, then, must Parigot report that recent years have seen the rapid disappearance of nearly all those delightful survivals of a lost leisure. Paris, be-

sieged, contained enough of them for all impractical
purposes. Then there were plenty of them still standing
groggily about for the melting armies of 1919 to roll
around in. But since then their number has greatly
and conspicuously diminished.

The greater hustle and bustle, the pressing, almost
panicky, sense of lost time which has visibly quickened
the very street scenes of England and France—that
may have had something to do with it. And the
wholesale demobilization of motors certainly did. The
poor old carriages were crowded out. What became
of them all? Did they journey in lonesome solemnity
to Père Lachaise, and vanish forever within its portals?
Did the *sapins* finally crumble to dust and the horses
lie down and die in the streets? I suspect so. Those
I knew were always threatening to do just that, even
in the tonic air of the Champs Elysées.

But while the *sapins* are almost all gone, many of the
*cochers* linger. The greater part of them have, it is
true, reluctantly discarded the costumes which made
them look as though they had been cut out of old
sporting prints. But they are still recognizable, sitting
bored and disdainful at the wheel of many a taxi, and,
what is more important, the fine tradition of the *cochers*
persists in all the taxi-stands within the fortifications.
The adventurous spirit, the imaginative driving, the
*esprit de corps*, manifested always in the unflagging
hostility which regarded all presumptive patrons

rather as presumptuous—that remains. Mr. Lucas of little faith might have known that even the taxis would be personal and picturesque in Paris. In Paris, and in Paris alone, taxi-driving is already a mellowed art. It would be so.

To consider the Parisian taxi-driver as an artist, it is only necessary to accept, without a struggle, the definition of an artist as one whose chief interest in his own work extends beyond any mere aspect of its advantage, assured or putative, financial or otherwise, to himself, and centers on the rôle of that work in the world. Of every job an artist undertakes, whether it be writing a novel or planting a bush, he asks: "What is this for?" rather than "What will this bring me?" By this standard your Parisian taxi-driver is indeed an artist, and it is only those zanies who do not know this that are forever becoming embroiled with him.

If you wish him to transport you, it is well not to rely on a mere display of wealth, either in your own habiliments or, more pointedly, by brandishing many notes of large denomination. He may be in communistic mood at the time. Watch that driver there, who seems so utterly indifferent to the frantic gestures of an imposing *Senateur*, yet who not only accepts as his fare an old market-woman but affably and ostentatiously assists her to stock his cab with enough panniers of vegetables to make it take on for a time the aspect of a huckster's cart.

Also, if you yourself happen to be a fat, wealthy, and rather offensive American tourist, remember of a Frenchman that his mere occupation and contentment with what may seem to you a menial task is no evidence that he is not a far more seasoned and cultivated gentleman than you are. I recall once asking a seedy driver if he knew, somewhere in the vicinity of the Trocadero, a street called the Rue du Tasse. "I know his verse, sir, but not his street," was the reply, which alternately stimulated and depressed me the rest of the day.

Then keep in mind that your driver may have been one of those who bore the reinforcements from the threatened city in the first battle of the Marne. At a recent reunion of them, one complained gayly that his meter had registered 675 francs when that great job was done, but that he had never been paid—complained gayly, mind you.

Above all, remember he is an artist. That is not to say that he is not often a very bad artist. Indeed, most of the Parisian drivers are execrable chauffeurs, moody, abstracted, fitful. They prefer a breakneck pace.

Once in pre-war days, when curiously bonneted women drivers were familiar sights at the taxi-wheels, I cried out to one in my dismay:

"Is there no speed limit in this mad city?"

"Oh, yes, monsieur," she answered sweetly over her shoulder, "but no one has ever succeeded in reaching it."

There is a legend that there are never any accidents, that the drivers proceed wildly through the swirl of traffic, grazing pedestrians on the Place Vendome, taking the Rivoli corner on one wheel, and careening toward the river, always coming within a hair's breadth of disaster, but always miraculously escaping. The legend is baseless. There are frequent crashes. If they are overlooked—as they certainly are in every chronicle of our time—it is, I think, because of the disarming glamour of human interest with which the drivers succeed in investing them.

Not long ago I saw two taxis collide at the right-bank end of the Pont Neuf, resulting in agitation and slight injury to the occupant of one of them, a stout matron whose false front somehow fitted in well with her jetty reticule, her shiny black valise, her three hat-boxes, and her Pekinese dog. These and she, all somewhat battered, adjourned with the floridly gesticulating drivers to the nearest *terrasse* for restoratives, and there they were soon surrounded by eleven policemen, most of them taking notes on the testimony. (I remember their exact number because it considerably embarrassed the waiter who was engaged at the time in illegally serving me cognac and coffee out of hours. Of course he went on serving it just the same, but it embarrassed him.) The discussion, which started with a warm controversy over this collision in particular and soon progressed to an experience meeting on collisions in general, then passed on to conversation on street-paving, automobile manufacture, and the venality and imcompetence of government, especially the present one. In this conference, the warring drivers, after exhausting the interest afforded by the spectacle of the swooning and slightly bloody lady, joined heartily, and for as much as an hour forewent their gainful occupation for its sake, while the original accident—its causes and its responsibility—was permanently forgotten.

These policemen were merely carrying on the tradition that traffic court should be held at once on the spot. Once when my taxi was hit by another with such violence that the chance companion sitting on the driver's seat of the offending cab was pitched out into the Place de la Concorde, I was greatly diverted to see him melt into the crowd and then, when court was held, emerge as a disinterested spectator who had just happened to witness the accident. His glib and imaginatively circumstantial testimony handsomely exonerated both drivers, and though a natural desire to have justice on the offending driver burned within *my* driver's heart, he was struck dumb with admiration for the style and ingenuity of the perjured witness. Oh, yes, all chroniclers to the contrary notwithstanding, they do have traffic disasters in the streets of Paris, but somehow the participants manage to make them more amusing and charming than anything else.

Bad artists, then, they often are, but artists always.

So, if you want them to trundle you about in times of stress, you must try to interest them in the purpose of your expedition. Remember that it is not possible to make a machine out of a Frenchman merely by putting him in one.

This key to the taxi-drivers of the boulevards rose in value in a certain year—1920—that severely strained the relations between them and the general public. Such strain would be inevitable in a time when petrol was so scarce, when *essence* was as costly as nectar. Then it was greatly aggravated by the disappearance of all small silver from circulation, what with the steady trickle of coins across the frontier and their inevitable concentration in the *chausettes* of a distrustful peasantry. The little packets of stamps, done up in paraffin paper and marked "1fr." or "2fr.," might circulate smoothly enough at the cafés and kiosks, even after some one had thought to depreciate the currency still further by extracting the contents of some of them. But they were poor things to brandish before a driver who was far from his own garage, who had very little gas left, who received no tip from his last customer, who was in pessimistic mood, and who was not really eager to take any one anywhere anyway.

Then the hostility was sharpened by the memories of two skirmishes. There was the strike of the drivers against the employing companies, which led, after much sarcasm, to a doubled tariff and was promptly followed by a popular boycott of the taxis, so that, for once in a way, the stands were always full. The sulky public, without visible or audible propaganda, declined to ride and for days persisted in their heroic refusal, days long to be remembered by those who actually saw the Parisian drivers gazing imploringly at pedestrian passersby. This really happened in several authenticated instances. It was a tremendous concession.

If you would know my hero at his best, you should hear the jovial Wythe Williams recount his adventures with him during the strike. That brief war emptied the streets except for the few driver-owned cabs, which cruised about the city enjoying not merely the opportunity for charging famine prices but also the innumerable chances of spurning uninteresting patrons. It was during such a conflict and on a night of fine drizzle which made the streets slippery and set all the gay river lights a-blinking, that Mr. and Mrs. Williams set forth after an early dinner at their apartment in the Rue Val du Grace, over by the *observatoire*. Theirs was the forlorn hope of being transported to the opera, a bad three miles away. They looked for a taxi, although the search for a magic carpet seemed just as feasible. They waved their umbrella at each of the few passing vehicles, only to be ignored.

One lone cab, its driver swathed in oilskins, his flag hooded, was loitering along the Boul' Miche', seemingly for the purpose of irritating whole sidewalks full of signaling pedestrians. One anxious native leaped on his running-board. "How much," he asked, "to the Gare d'Orsay?" "A hundred francs," replied the driver with mischievous gravity and then chuckled delightedly at the fellow's collapse.

Suddenly he beheld the forlorn Williamses, clad for the opera, and huddled pathetically at the curb under the family umbrella. Something smote him. He circled over to within hailing distance.

"Where do you want to go?" he roared.

"To the opera," they replied miserably.

"To the opera itself?"

They nodded assent.

"My God, sir!" he cried, "it's 'Samson' to-night, with a ballet afterward—one of those double bills, very long. It will begin early. Don't you know you'll be late?"

They admitted that it seemed dismally probable.

"Well, well," he went on impatiently, and with no descent to barter, though the opportunity was rich, "jump in, jump in! There's no time to lose."

Through the deserted streets they rocked and skidded, crossed the river like one streak, skirted the Louvre in death-defying fashion, and swept along the streaming avenue, just as the clock there at the Boulevard des Italiens pointed to 7:45.

"Thank God," he wheezed as they piled out, "we are in time for the overture."

I don't know how much Williams paid him. Enough, I hope, to add appreciably to the sum he was surely saving to buy up a certain morsel of land in his own *pays*, where he would grow his own haricots verts, eat them, and live to be a hundred and two.

It is comparatively easy to negotiate for a brief trip along the boulevards. It requires no art to engage a taxi from the Madeleine, say, to the showy office of the Matin. But my precepts become valuable when you aspire to some distant goal. You need all your wiles and a good deal of currency, for instance, to be taken to the Butte Montmartre, the peak of that solitary hill whose strangely Byzantine cathedral, opalescent at sundown, greets from afar the eyes of all pilgrims whose feet are turned toward Paris. In the crazy old houses clustered like beggars around its gates some of the best cooks in France practise their art. *Soufflées* of singular delicacy and unforgetable *ragoûts* reward the wise men who make the ascent. But it *IS* a fearful ascent and the taxis avoid it, even when insulted with extraordinary bribes. Usually a *pourboire* of exceptional and specified proportions is not enough to take you past the foot of the asthmatic *funiculaire* which, for a small consideration, will attend to the rest.

That is why I was surprised once when I appealed to a sad-eyed, bewhiskered driver to take me to the Butte—all the way to the Butte, to the very edge of Turtle Square, I explained—and he neither fainted nor roared with laughter as all others had done. He merely looked at me with a curiously troubled and wistful expression in his eyes.

"Turtle Square?" he repeated nervously.

"It's not so very far," I lied urgently.

"Oh," he replied at once, "it's not that. Jump in."

So away we rattled, the engine protesting raucously every foot of the way.

Once arrived at the Café of the Happy Mill (the soiled one opposite the entrance to old St. Pierre), and I had paid him, he made no move to go but just sat and stared and stared. I felt guiltily that he thought of me as having tricked him into a difficult and unprofitable journey.

"Haven't you ever been here before?" I asked loftily in what I fondly imagined were the accents of a born Parisian.

"Not for many, many years," he replied gravely. "That's why I hesitated to come. I haven't been back here since they dispossessed me from my little café. It was the night the score of 'Louise' was played for the first time at that studio there, around the corner and across the square. It all looks just the same," he concluded, and eyed me appealingly as if he hoped that in some way I would show him it had all changed for the worse.

"Will you have an *aperitif*, my friend?" I ventured, and so we sat in silence at the nearest table while he drained a glass to his bitter-sweet memories. Then he wiped his eyes of two unabashed tears, cranked up his dilapidated car, waved to me in mute farewell, and drove off down toward the boulevards, without once turning his head.

But the driver who taught me most was the one from whom I first learned the trick (since practised with unvarying success) of being transported at the legal rates to my hotel on the Isle de Cité. That hotel is called the City Hotel, and for various reasons, not all of them financial, I like to stop there. LeRoy Baldridge, the artist, discovered it first. I think he just dropped in to ask the *patronne* why she had not called it the Commercial House, and installed a sample room while she was about it. But during the ensuing banter he became sufficiently interested in the place to move in. It is several hundred years old and has only one bathtub, but, as I never knew this to be used by any other guest, the illusion of a private bath was almost perfect. I liked my old room there because, from its balcony, I could throw my cigarette-butts into the Seine, a thrilling privilege, I should think, for any one with an atom of historical sense.

The hotel stands at the tip of that island which was the beginning of Paris, just where it bisects the Pont Neuf, so that its windows look down on the bridge, and give a heartening view of Henri Quatre as he sits astride his bronze horse across the roadway.

Among its other advantages it may be said of this hotel that no one under any circumstances knows where it is. Its obscure street-number means nothing in the lives of Parisian chauffeurs. Thus it happened that one stormy night—it was really one stormy morning—when I approached a taxi by the *Étoile* in an effort to be carried home, I merely said to the driver: "Will you take me to the middle of the Pont Neuf?"

I suppose my inner conviction that he would do nothing of the kind tinged my voice with melancholy. He looked at me with sudden and vivid interest.

"What," he asked in a sort of stage-whisper, "would take you to such a place at such an hour? The middle of the Pont Neuf at two in the morning! My God!"

Instantly I realized that he had forgotten all about the island which the Pont Neuf crosses, forgotten entirely the few buildings which abutt upon its footway. I could see that he pictured me as poised, sad but resolute, in the middle of the bridge on a night of storm. The prospect excited him enormously. He repeated his question in tones even more sombre. "What errand takes you there?"

I choked back my rising laughter, and in accents as tragic as his own replied: "That, my old one, is my business. Drive on."

And, still under the spell of this drama, he lifted his hands to high heaven, forgot all about my stipulation as to fare, waved for me to get in, and drove off at a speed which seemed nicely to compromise between the urgency of his curiosity and his instinct for an appropriately funereal pace. I shall carry to my grave, which I trust will be no watery one after all, the memory of his startled face as I hopped cheerfully out in the middle of the bridge and bent under the light of his wet lamp to count out his three francs. His glance, as it took in the dim outline of the hotel on the forgotten island, was one of mingled incredulity and indignation. He was both chuckling and cursing as he drove off hurriedly toward the right bank—a bloodthirsty fellow, a bit of a brigand, I suppose, but for all that a fellow liberal, an individualist, and an artist.

# MRS. FISKE

ONE fine day, St. John Ervine said to himself: "Be jocund, chuck," or words to that effect. Doubtless he felt that in "John Ferguson," "Jane Clegg," and "Mixed Marriages," he had had enough for the nonce, of murder, theft, rape, bigotry, parental sternness, and all such dourer aspects of the human comedy.

"I will be frivolous. This young Mr. Milne is frivolous, so why not I? I will frolic. Go to, I will be gay."

So saying he retired to his typewriter and thought for twenty minutes. What, he asked himself, is the most amusing thing I can possibly imagine? He thought for another twenty minutes, and then wrote out a sentence which, perhaps, ran something in this wise: "Just suppose Mrs. Pat Campbell were to spend the week-end at a chaste, calm old vicarage in the heart of the English countryside!"

This supposition proved too much for Mr. Ervine's sense of gravity, and straightway he dashed off the play called "Mary, Mary, Quite Contrary." In it a florid, capricious actress falls on a quiet, rural household like a mediæval calamity, passes through it with some of the upsetting tendencies usually ascribed to typhoons, and moves on in a cloud of dust, leaving its exhausted but stimulated people to live on the memory of her visit all the days of their lives.

It was this manuscript which fell into the hands of David Belasco one fine June day, and it was with this play that he reopened his theater a year later; reopened it with more than the usual flourish because, during the Summer, he had persuaded Mrs. Fiske to impart her vivacity, her charm, her style, and her unquenchable gayety to the amusing rôle of *Mary Westlake*. The first New York performance was a glowing one, and the Belasco Theater, in all its nights, was never quite so full of chuckles.

It is easy to guess that the far away Mr. Ervine had in mind a rather different actress—one younger, more opulent, more languorous, more like a slightly damaged full-blown rose. In the theater of his mind, as he wrote, it is improbable that he saw any one so nervous, so darting, so brittle, so gleaming as Minnie Maddern Fiske.

On the other hand, it is even easier to guess that, with an ordinary actress in the title rôle, Mr. Ervine's comedy would have seemed a rather panting and elephantine frolic, as insipid a draught as the lukewarm juice of pressed parsnips.

It so happened that his play was touched by the most electric hand in the theater. The result was as festive and enjoyable a first night as we have attended in years. In "Mary, Mary, Quite Contrary," Mrs. Fiske gave a performance of incomparable brilliance and charm, and the first New York audience that welcomed her was so glad to see her again, so responsive to the nudge of her comedy, so warm with affection for her, that before the evening was half spent, one had the illusion that a thousand friends were carrying her in triumph on their shoulders.

First nights tread so fast on one another's heels in Manhattan, that it is rare for one of them to seem eventful. There has been a perceptible change since the days when Poe was a dramatic critic and went to the first twenty-two performances of Anna Cora Mowatt's "Fashion" at the old Park because there were no other plays for him to see. Now the arrival of a new play on Broadway causes about as much excitement as the arrival of a new baby at a Maternity Hospital. There are times when only the father and mother seem really interested. But now and again, as when a Barrymore plays "Hamlet" or when a "First Year" comes unexpectedly through the fog, an old festivity is recaptured. It is heart warming.

Among those visibly happy on this occasion, mention might be made of David Belasco. His habitually benign expression was complicated by faint traces of the enigmatic look usually associated with the cat that has swallowed the canary. In the loveliest tale told

by the late Maurice Hewlett, a young knight rode into
a mysterious forest, dauntless with this device: "I bide
my time." Mr. Belasco might have written that legend
on his own shield that night, for the coming of "Mary,
Mary" to his theater was the ending of a chapter that
had been left unfinished forty years before.

It was back in his leanest years that he first gave
himself over to blandishments intended to woo Mrs.
Fiske under his management. He was a young and
obscure free lance in the theater—playwright, actor,
director, or "what have you?"—who was working his
way East from San Francisco, bent on taking the $35
a week job that had been offered him as manager of
the old Madison Square. A new crony of his at that
time was another young adventurer who was junketing
up and down the country as manager of Haverley's
Minstrels. Each had grandiose plans for the future
and, since the model was then Augustin Daly, each felt
the acute need of finding an Ada Rehan at once.

It must have been with some such notion in the back
of his head that the threadbare but aspiring Belasco
made up his mind one night to go back stage and present
himself to the saucy and beguiling newcomer who was
playing in a fearful melodrama at the Park Theater, in
Boston. Her name was Minnie Maddern, and the piece
was a gaudy and violent variant of the "Peg o' My
Heart" species. *Its* name was "Fogg's Ferry" and,
except for a recent brief resuscitation it has since owed

to the omnivorous movies, it vanished from sight after serving its purpose—that of bringing East a startling and sprightly soubrette, in whom show folk everywhere were interested because she was the sixteen-year-old daughter of Tom Davey and Lizzie Maddern.

In "Fogg's Ferry" (a really choice script, bejewelled with such haughty lines as "Pardon me, I had not noticed there was a menial present"), it was the agreeable duty of Miss Maddern to wear very short skirts, sit on a table, sing and, at one crisis, crawl out on a ledge and save a treasure-laden steamship by firing a revolver at the bomb which lay in wait for it in the river's bed.

It was on the ascendant young star of this lusty entertainment that Belasco was minded to call. Because he wanted to be free to do so without competition, he was delighted to find that his crony had a project of his own for that evening. Belasco was even pleased to finance that project, whatever it might be, by making the then prodigious loan of two dollars. This, it seems, was not his total capital; for, as soon as he was alone, he hied him to a florist's and bought as imposing a bouquet as he could find. Reinforced with this, he repaired to the Park Theater to take the first step in his campaign.

What first froze him to the ground and then galvanized him into sudden and even violent action, was the sight of a rival turning into the stage door alley just ahead of him. It was a rival, also reinforced with flowers—flowers, which, as Belasco had bitter reason to know, must have cost two dollars.

There followed then in the alley a magnificent fight, the two young adventurers rolling over and over together, with at least one of the bouquets quite hopelessly involved in the scrimmage. You must picture this scene, lit by a wind-tossed gas jet and vastly enjoyed by the entire company, which came trouping out still in costume to see what all the ructions were about. It was most enjoyed, no doubt, by young Miss Maddern herself, whom you can see bobbing up and down with excitement, laughing behind her inevitable fan, and insisting from time to time that taller folk must not obscure her view of what, after all, was *her* fight. It was she who had perpetrated it, however innocently, and its thrills were chiefly hers to enjoy.

It seems to have been a sufficiently hearty contest to have suspended negotiations indefinitely, and it was years before she saw either of the two again. Indeed, it was not until ten years ago, or thereabouts, that she saw one of them next. He was frail and lame then, and he hobbled back stage to see her when she was playing at the Hudson Theater in "The High Road." His name was Charles Frohman. At the first sight of her, he grinned.

"Did you keep the flowers, Minnie Maddern?" he asked.

"Dear Mr. Frohman," she said and held out both her hands in the loveliest gesture of welcome and regret, "would that I could have!"

After all, it was Belasco who won.

One who greatly enjoyed the result, one who laughed and who, indeed, felt himself moved almost to get up and make a speech on the opening night of "Mary, Mary, Quite Contrary," can still recognize that such a dramatic antic is not worth a whole season of this magnificent actress's time, and can regret every week wasted when she is away from the great rôles to which she has seemed destined.  One of these, that of *Mrs. Malaprop*, she seems likely to play before so very long. The other, *Lady Macbeth*, she will probably never attempt.  Yet what a *Lady Macbeth* she would make; what an intense and tortured *Lady Macbeth*, with what an inner flame!

She has never played *Lady Macbeth*, and it is some years since she has appeared in the play at all.  Indeed, it was at the age of three or thereabouts that she put the nursery behind her and assumed the rôle of the crowned child in the caldron scene, when Barry Sullivan was playing "Macbeth" in New Orleans.  It was her task to rise through the steam and buoy up the faltering King with these words:

"Oh, fret not where conspirers are!"

Only, she said "perspirers," an unpremeditated textual change which had so startling an effect on the star that it was found necessary to ring down the curtain. There may have been some doubt that evening as to whether the new Maddern would ever amount to much in the theater, but I predict a great future for her.

Indeed, in any repertory of Mrs. Fiske's, I should like to see not only "Macbeth" and "The Rivals," but Ibsen's "Ghosts" and "The Lady From the Sea" and Chekhov's "The Cherry Orchard." Some of us will never be quite happy until she has played *Mrs. Malaprop*, preferably with Frank Craven as *Bob Acres* and William Harrigan as *Sir Lucius O'Trigger*. She would be superb as the vague, tearful, helpless, pretty mother in "The Cherry Orchard."

And while the subject is up, it might as well be suggested that all the playwrights who have always had it in mind to write a rôle for Mrs. Fiske might do well to bestir themselves. There are two such rôles we should like to have attended to at once. Notice is hereby served on Messrs. Forbes, Kaufman, Connelly, Moeller, et al., that a favorable review is assured for a comedy dealing with life in a theatrical boarding house off Union Square in 1890, with W. C. Fields cast as a tragedian out of work and Mrs. Fiske installed as a whilom Shakespearean actress who, though she has forsaken the bard for the securer emoluments of a boarding house keeper, still employs the grand manner for the serving of prunes.

Then notice is served on Edward Sheldon, G. K. Chesterton and any others who feel equal to it that there is a fine play yet to be written about one who was the great lady of Paris before ever the Normans battered at its gates. Most of us who know Sainte Geneviève at all know her from the murals which spell out her story on the walls of the Pantheon—from the cool, brooding Puvis de Chauvannes picture, which shows her standing guard at night over the sleeping city, a tranquil picture which is in itself a benediction, to the more colorful and larger canvas which shows the old woman grandly dying, with all Paris on its knees from her bedside to the river's edge.

It is possible that, to the heathen student, the child Geneviève partakes a little too much of the persnicketty quality of *Elsie Dinsmore*, particularly in the episode wherein her mother strikes her for loitering at church and is therefore turned blind and left blind until the forgiving child's prayers restore her eyesight—eighteen months later. But all of us can join in an enjoyment of Geneviève in her later years, when she bossed the city, defending it in time of siege and revictualing it under the very noses of the Huns by sneaking down the river to Chalons, doing a few healings in return for grain and smuggling eleven boatloads of it back to the beleaguered city, where she kept an eye on the shiftless housewives to see that they did not waste it in baking cakes. As she grew older her spell grew more potent and it was in a very panic for her health that the bishops met and ordered her to enlarge her diet beyond the few

lentils and water she considered quite sufficient. When
the barbarians finally did get through the gate it was
not until they had made their terms with her—not,
in fact, until after she had hobbled out to meet them,
cracked their heads together and baptized them then
and there.

I should like to send a few playwrights to the Pantheon, bid them study the paintings of her and meditate
a while on this old Frenchwoman of such spirit that for
a thousand years after her death the people of her city
felt more comfortable in time of danger if her bones
were lifted from the crypt and carried through the
streets as a talisman against all that could work them
ill. Then perhaps some day we should have the pleasure
of going to a theater to see Mrs. Fiske as *Mrs. Malaprop*
and reading in the program a quiet note which
would say—Wednesday, Thursday and Friday nights
and Saturday matinée "Geneviève," by Edward
Sheldon.

In the excellent company Mr. Belasco rounded up
for "Mary, Mary, Quite Contrary" there was, by the
way, one actor concerning whom there is this legend.
It seems he was to make his first appearance in a play
in London and as he was entering the cast late in the run
he was smitten by the horrid possibility that news of
the début might not get around. So he wired wildly
in every direction, announcing to managers, playwrights and critics his advent in such and such a rôle

on such and such a night.  All of his sheaf of telegrams
elicited only one response.  It was as follows:

> " Dear Sir:
>   " Thanks for the warning.
>                            " J. M. BARRIE."

It was during the run of "Mary, Mary" at the
Belasco that some of us, wishing to lure Mrs. Fiske
to a party, racked our brains to concoct the kind of
festivity she would most enjoy.  There is a tavern
in our town which was a tavern when New York was
an English colony.  Before its cozy fires the officers
of King George's army lounged in comfort while
Washington's men were stamping up and down in the
snow at Valley Forge.  It was in its long room one flight
up from the street that Washington himself said farewell to his own officers a few years later, and it was
its innkeeper whom Washington summoned to Philadelphia as steward of the first Presidential mansion
before ever the White House was built or even planned.
The tavern was called Fraunces, and it still stands at
Broad and Pearl, and still, as in 1770, can be engaged
of an evening "for the Polite and Rational Entertainment of Philosophical Lectures, &c."

No one now alive in the service of the old inn could
recall its ever having been open of a Sunday until this
Sunday evening when the fires were laid and the lamps
lit while in the little ground floor room, whose windows

look out on Pearl Street, a dinner was being held in honor of the first lady of the theater.

It was Edna Ferber, Neysa McMein, Alice Duer Miller, Father Duffy, Franklin P. Adams and your humble servant who, when the time came, 'drank the toast to Mrs. Fiske. That toast was blandly proposed by Robert C. Benchley, who stammered a good deal, murmuring vague somethings about life and the long road—as Wordsworth so beautifully expressed it. Or was it Bossuet? Thus he rambled on, beaming amiably at the ceiling and sitting down at last without having mentioned Mrs. Fiske at all.

That touch, perhaps, was not unplanned. Planned certainly was the leisurely approach to the tavern. Through Trinity's churchyard, filled with a gentle melancholy in the late October sunlight. Through Battery Park, which, when the mist is on the sea and a new risen moon is in the sky, has a thousand earnests of romance. As you look out at M. Bartholdi's handiwork thus shrouded and see the little ships emerge silent from the gathering dusk you became vaguely conscious that on a Sunday evening the Battery is wistful with a great nostalgia. And you guess that the few silent folk who share the benches with you have come down to ease an intolerable homesickness by staring out to sea.

Then there are the mysterious caverns to be visited, the dark caves of Wall Street and Nassau and Exchange

Place, with the lights gone now and the myriad windows and the scuffle from their footways. Indeed you have not savored the mystery of that deserted city until you have heard the echo of your own horse's hoofbeats on the empty asphalt. That was why it was so thoughtful of Brother Benchley to come to the rescue of one pilgrim who had so far forgotten the spirit of the occasion as to come down in some such paltry modern conveyance as a motor car. But that she might not miss the great effect he obligingly raced up and down Wall Street beating earnestly on the sidewalk with his stick.

However, it was the uninvited guests who gave the happiest fillip to the party. There were four of them, aged each about 9 years or 10. Attracted by the light at the open window they climbed on the ledge and presented four interested faces as a sort of chorus to the dinner. An equitable division of the after dinner mints quite won their hearts, but they were less responsive when, perhaps forgetting for the moment that she was no longer involved in "Wake Up, Jonathan," Mrs. Fiske took four red roses from the table and proffered them as something to be taken home to their mothers.

"No," said their spokesman firmly, and when Lady Bountiful looked a trifle abashed he explained kindly, "I *work* in a florist's."

But they were not unappreciative of the peppermints,

and before they bore them off into the darkness the smallest boy leaned way into the room and said:

"Thank you, one and all, gentlemen and women of leisure."

# MR. TARKINGTON

THIS chapter may set forth bravely enough as an account of a delightful and unsuccessful comedy called "Tweedles" but it really aims to say something about Booth Tarkington. "Tweedles" was an amused scrutiny of family pride woven around a youthful romance of the Maine coast. Such was its flavor that when we cruised out into the night after its first New York performance we passed by a snappy young taxi in favor of a lazy, old Victoria. Furthermore, as the rheumatic but dignified horse clop-clop-clopped along the night-cooled asphalt, our thoughts were turned back beyond "Tweedles" to another comedy, which, if not the best, was certainly the dearest of our time. That was "A Kiss for Cinderella," by J. M. Barrie.

You may remember the curious quality which *Mr. Bodie* noticed in *Cinderella* as she came in each day to dust his studio. "I can't help liking her," he would say. "She's so extraordinarily *homely* that you can't be with her many minutes before you begin thinking of your early days. Where were you born, officer?"

"I'm from Badgery," said the infallible policeman stifly.

"She'll make you think of Badgery," Mr. Bodie warned him.

"She'd best try no games on me," replied the policeman grimly.

But she did. Indeed, a few moments later when he caught and cross-questioned her, the process began. He was about to make a powerful impression on her when he was conscious of her embarrassing scrutiny directed toward the middle of his person.

"Now then," he broke in fiercely, "what are you staring at?"

CINDERELLA (*hotly*)—That's a poor way to polish a belt. If I was a officer I would think shame of having my belt in that condition.

POLICEMAN (*undoubtedly affected by her homeliness but unconscious of it*)—It's easy to speak; it's a miserable polish, I admit, but mind you, I'm pretty done when my job's over; and I have the polishing to do myself.

CINDERELLA—You have no woman person?

POLICEMAN—Not me.

CINDERELLA (*with passionate arms*)—If I had that belt for half an hour!

POLICEMAN—What would you use?

CINDERELLA—Spit.

POLICEMAN—Spit? That's like what my mother would have said. That was in Badgery, where I was born. When I was a boy at Badgery—(*He stops short. She had reminded him of Badgery*).

CINDERELLA—What's wrong?

POLICEMAN (*heavily*)—How did you manage that about Badgery?

CINDERELLA—What?

POLICEMAN—Take care, prisoner.

Yet when he came to woo her in the final scene you may be sure it was as one who told how the heart of him cried out to walk with her beside Badgery water.

Is it an idle fancy to suggest that something of this gift which *Cinderella* had is among the many possessed by Booth Tarkington? You can't be many minutes with his books and plays before you begin thinking of your early days. Just as certain weddings in New York bring out onto the highways a type of inhabitant most of us never see here from one year's end to another, just as even several years ago you had to sit down and look about you in a Maude Adams audience to be reminded from time to time how many delightful people still lived in New York, so the plays and books of Booth Tarkington not only set astir a thousand memories of an America that was, but what is more important, suggest to those of us who live in exile here that that America continues.

We who have season seats on the enchanted aisles and review one by one the hundreds of plays which come here to bid for favor each year are in sore need of such reassurance. One summer in an issue of the

*Smart Set* (the December number, doubtless) Mr. Mencken, in enlarging upon a new guide book to New York, reported that the reading of it made his conscience toss and grunt a bit, "for the fact is borne upon me that, despite my long familiarity with New York, I really know nothing about the town. The truth is that, like most other persons who visit it regularly and like many who live in it, I confine my habitual travels in it to a very limited area. The region between Forty-second Street on the south, Forty-fifty Street on the north, Fifth Avenue on the east and Sixth Avenue on the west I know pretty well—well enough, indeed, to navigate it day or night without lights. It is within that rectangle that I sleep when I am in New York, and there I have my office and eat most of my meals. What lies outside is, in the main, mysterious to me, though I have been making trips around the town for twenty-five years."

But Brother Mencken is a commuter. He lives in Baltimore, where the sight of him watering his geraniums and guarding his own cellar is among the reassuring entertainments afforded by that city. But those of us who act as scouts for you among the new plays are for the most part resident members of his little rectangle or, at most, of an area centering there and stretching not much further. Small wonder if, from time to time, we in our dependence on books and plays for knowledge of life in America, find ourselves believing that that life now swings inevitably from the dull, fly specked routine of Gopher Prairie as Sinclair Lewis saw it to the gaudier didoes of Long Island as the Hattons recalled them.

To such exiles the Tarkington works (right down to "The Fascinating Stranger" and "Tweedles") come with a renovating force. The fabric of American life as he sees it—the hum of distant lawn-mowers whirring through summer air, the swish of garden hose playing at sundown on phlox and petunia and heliotrope, the sound of neighbor calling to neighbor, the fragrance of new made bread sifting from sunny kitchens, the slow, ritualistic mastication of Sunday dinners at grandma's, the tattered bound volumes of *St. Nicholas Magazine* still within reach in the bookcases in case you should want to verify something in "Davy and the Goblin," the whisper of courtship on vine hung verandas, the clatter of a Ramsey Milholland's strapful of books on the white palings as he passes by on his way from school —these and a hundred reminiscent sounds and colors and smells, these and the far more telling things that the people of his stories say and do and are, these as part of his own accent and viewpoint somehow tell you in their way that the essence of the America for which Louisa Alcott wrote and which bred Richard Watson Gilder and William Dean Howells and Kate Douglas Wiggin, is an essence still distilled. It is in the overtones of "Tweedles." Listen intently and you will hear it.

"Tweedles" is a good humored comedy of family pride. Its great moment is reached in the second act, when the *Rockmores* of Germantown (or whatever the name is of the complacent Philadelphians in this case) arrive majestically to halt the budding romance between their Willie Baxterish son and the gentle *Winsora*. *Winsora* is the bright, ginghamy daughter of a homespun native named *Tweedle*. The Philadelphians know him only as a capable carpenter who has done some odd jobs for them about their summer place in Maine. They do not know that the *Tweedles* have dwelt there in season and out for two hundred years and are as puffed up about it as the *Rockmores* are about their place in West Walnut Lane. And the supreme moment comes when it is borne painfully in on these Ritzy visitors that the *Tweedles* have no mind to let their daughter throw herself away on a mere summer person from God knows where—that the *Tweedles*, in short, do not consider the *Rockmores* good enough for them.

The young romance was safely left to Gregory Kelly and Ruth Gordon, both charming and capable young players for whom the piece was written—or at least, rewritten. Miss Gordon's performance was a really glowing one. Then there was a gorgeous character study of a Maine type by Donald Meek, at which the first audience fairly roared with joy. But the burden of the chief scene fell on one George Farren as *Tweedle*, pere, who bore up splendidly under it.

When the play was given in Chicago the preceding season under the name of "Bristol Glass," this part was entrusted to Frank McGlynn, fresh from two years of touring in "Abraham Lincoln." The legend is that he was so saturated in that tragedy that he could not help imparting a note of impending doom to the Tarkington-Wilson gayeties.

"Indeed," some one said later, "McGlynn played the whole second act as if he knew Booth were going to kill him in the third."

"Nonsense," put in the adjacent G. S. K., "Tarkington wouldn't kill even an actor."

In the somewhat muddy account of that first night as recorded in our journal next day, there occurred this paragraph:

"At some stage in its evolution, Harry Leon Wilson entered in, for, as in the days when the two of them collaborated so prosperously on 'The Man From Home,' so now in this new comedy of youthful love and family pride, their names are linked upon the program. Yet, if memory serves, there was no mention of Mr. Wilson's having had a hand in the business when this play was forecast a full two years ago, nor any mention of him when, under the name of 'Bristol Glass,' it was proffered tentatively to Chicago last season. One is permitted to suspect if not to announce that he was called in for the overhauling of a piece which had been left for an unaccountably long time on the shelf and which had not been precisely stampeded with popular approval in Chicago."

It might as well be admitted that this bit of literary divination was set down with something of the aplomb of the student, who, after looking fiercely at three lines of "Othello," is able to announce that it was written by Queen Elizabeth. We felt like Mr. Holmes when he would scrape up a bit of ash from the sidewalk and decide at once that the murderer was a nearsighted man from Utah suffering from chilblains. "Nothing more revelatory than cigar ash, my dear Watson. There are 756 sharply differentiated kinds. You must read a little monograph I wrote on the subject."

Next day, however, we had time to resort to the more ingenious detective method of asking some one who knew. It then appeared that everything in the paragraph was precisely wrong. Mr. Tarkington and Mr. Wilson had written the play together in Maine three or four summers before and the rewriting was done by Mr. Tarkington in the interval.

AT some time in the writing of "Mary the Third"
we suspect that Rachel Crothers was minded to call
this sometimes delightful comedy of hers "The Sofa."
It is the sofa which played chorus, or could play chorus,
to the unfolding of the play. It was on the sofa during
a dance one night in 1870 that the lovely, twittering,
curl bedecked *Mary* of that period sat and tapped her
fan to the strains of "The Blue Danube" sifting in from
the orchestra, and planned how, in a determined but
maidenly manner, she would detach a young plutocrat
from the clutches of her dear little friend *Lucy* and
elope with him on Firefly, then champing the bit under
the oak tree down the lane.

It was on the same sofa, reupholstered, that *Mary's*
ravishing daughter negotiated her own marriage at a
dance in the same house twenty-seven years later. It
was all managed to the tune of the latest Sousa march,
which was providing a hoppy two step for the dancers
out on the floor. This was a *Mary* clad in a blue silk
gown that broke out in little balloons just below the
shoulder and expanded over wide hips where the full

skirt hitched itself on to the long waisted bodice. It was a *Mary* that flirted her tasseled dance card a trifle less coquettishly, a *Mary* whose high piled coiffure caught the eye with a pompadour built over a rat. Her swains, clad in clawhammer coats, look now as though they had just stepped down from a fading banquet picture. As they wait for her in the play one of them, the dude of the two, tweaks the other by singing softly:

> Daisy, Daisy, give me your answer true,
> I'm half crazy all for the love of you,
> It won't be a stylish marriage,
> We can't afford a carriage,
> But you'll look sweet
> Upon the seat
> Of a bicycle built for two.

As we recall the modes of the day, it was considered the clever thing to hold onto the "two" in the last line of that chorus and glide at once into "Two Little Girls in Blue," the song with a plot so involved that we never could follow it. But surely, Miss Crothers, your up-and-coming lad of 1897 was not still singing that song. He was more likely to sing "I Guess I'll Have to Telegraph My Baby," which a youngster named George Cohan had written, or to hum the refrain of "Follow On," which a lovely newcomer named Edna May was singing in New York. However, *Mary the Third* wouldn't know. Not the keen, pretty *Mary* of 1923, whose cigarette burns holes in the new covering of the sofa the while she worries her mother and horrifies her grandmother by proclaiming in advance her convictions, as an outsider looking in, that marriage is a dull and slightly disgusting institution.

We take inordinate interest in any play written in the "Milestones" manner, as "Secrets" is, and to a lesser extent "Mary the Third." We go on hoping from season to season that before long one of our playwrights will write a comedy woven entirely out of his memories of what it was like to live in this country twenty-five years ago. It is such a meager glimpse that we got of "The Sporting Widow Brown" in the Greenwich Village Follies. It was such a flying visit we paid to the 1897 of "Mary the Third." And for the most part our playwrights avoid as pestilential the fertile field stretching between "Time—the Present" and "When Grandma Was a Girl." Yet we yearn to see a comedy called "In 1897" to match the poem called "In 1889," by Vachel Lindsay. Arthur Richman might turn his hand to it and emerge with something named "Not So Long Ago as That Even." Edna Ferber could do it after her tour de force of reconstruction in "The Girls," but her own memories of that year would be those of a bouncing ten-year-old girl known to the neighbors in Appleton, Wis., as Fluff. In fact, we would be inclined to turn the whole matter over to the man who wrote "The Magnificent Ambersons." Mr. Tarkington would have the time of his life reaching back for 1897 and holding it for a few hours for our amused recollection. It would be recapturing a period little more distant in time from us than was the New York of "Captain Jinks," when Clyde Fitch wrote the comedy which introduced the willowy Ethel Barrymore in crinolines, or the America of "Shenandoah," when Bronson Howard dramatized the Civil War.

"In 1897" would have as its background the prosperous country over which William McKinley presided amiably, a country all the roads of which were dotted with bicycles and every soda water fountain had a rack for them on the sidewalk outside. It must, indeed, make a good deal out of the inveterate bicycle rider, especially the one who was referred to as a "scorcher" and whose handle bars were so low that every one was sure he would soon expire of curvature of the spine. Indeed, riding with low handle bars was vaguely associated with deviltry as jazz dancing is to-day, and his elders were convinced that he would come to a bad end. And wasn't it in 1897 that young folk became aware that folding beds were not quite the thing? And modish daughters persuaded their astonished parents that the once-admired patent rocker ought to be moved up out of the parlor into the sewing room, where no one ever went except Aunt Millie when she came on a visit.

We read "Quo Vadis" and "The Martian" in those days and devoured the newspaper accounts of Victoria's

Jubilee, and of the gold that was being unearthed up in the Klondike. If we were in New York, stopping at the Holland House or the Fifth Avenue Hotel, we drove up town in the evening to see the new risen star named Maude Adams, who was appearing at the Empire in "The Little Minister," under the management of one of those brothers whom the uncomprehending Ada Rehan was referring to disdainfully as "these Frohmans." At home the grownups played duplicate whist or progressive euchre and the kids gathered under the lamppost at the corner to compare their collections of those white celluloid buttons which one wore on the lapel with those of more indecent import hidden underneath to be exposed only furtively. The girls spent untold hours copying Gibson heads and framing them in passe-partout as Christmas gifts, and grandma shook her head sadly over the coarse tendency to shout "Nit" and "Rubber" manifested by the younger generation. The really smart fellow was the swagger one who was beginning to appear at the beaches and golf courses (golf was coming in) minus his coat and, wonder of wonders, minus his suspenders. (But Mr. Tarkington may not use the bold Shirt Waist Man in this play of ours because Marc Connelly already has him in mind for some scene of his own concoction.)

It was quite a long time ago—1897. Woodrow Wilson had just been appointed professor of politics at Princeton and the ex-Crown Prince of Germany was a dear little lad over whose prowess at school and whose innocent pastimes there used to be gushing articles in *Harper's Young People*—no, it was *Harper's Round Table* by that time. We gathered that there never had been such a fine, manly, upstanding little chap in all the world, and it was made pretty clear to us what a well trained monarch he would be if, as the articles said, "God spared him to rule over his great, peace loving people." Our worries were more about Spain, whose gouty hand still held the struggling Cubans, and our agitation on that subject was causing a good deal of indignation in Berlin. "If more sober after-thought does not dam the stream of American Chauvinism," said a Berlin editorial, "we Germans shall not feel sorry in the event that the Americans finally reach a sounder judgment relative to their powers: *i.e.*, if they got a drubbing to teach them that nobody may brandish a pistol with impunity." It was the end of an era—the last of the America that knew not automobiles, movies and opera in the home and did not remember the taste of foreign blood. Yes, 1897 was quite a long time ago.

After we had, as a matter of fact, duly instructed Mr. Tarkington and George Ade to write "In 1897," both of them declined firmly, both discouraged by their adventures in the theater and, at the moment, minded never to write for it again. Mr. Ade's refusal came in the form of a letter from Florida.

"I wish I could do it," he wrote, "but I have taken
the veil and retired to a monastery and I am a playwright no longer. Possibly I never was one. I refer
you to Alan Dale. The full bloom of my recollections
would center around the eighties instead of the nineties
and some time when I am full of ambition I will write
you something about the days when 'The Mikado'
and the pompadour and the skin tight trousers ruled
the world." A disposition to question the archæologi-
cal soundness of any one who puts "The Mikado"
and the pompadour into the same era was lost in the
desolation induced by this announcement that Mr.
Ade would not write for the theater at all. It still seems
too monstrous that the author of "The College Widow"
and "The County Chairman" should call it a day when
we consider all the prolific playwrights of to-day who
could get them to a monastery this afternoon without
wringing a single tear from us.

# STEPHEN CRANE

THE foolish little moment of 1897 that tripped to the measure of a Sousa march in the play called "Mary the Third," the glimpse of 1900 and 1901, which next enlivened certain scenes in "The Lady" at the Empire, even the shrewd understanding glance down the years which Edna Ferber afforded in the extraordinary vistas of "The Girls"—none of these does more than hint at that recreation of the sound and look and accent of the '90s, which some of us feel that a Tarkington (as if there were several Tarkingtons) might mold into a true retrospective play of American life. Unexpectedly enough, the best promise of it lies unspoken between the lines of a book which started out to be a loving biography of Stephen Crane and turned out to be not only that but a far from loving study of an America that was. Thomas Beer wrote it. It is, on both scores, the most enthralling book which 1923 brought this way.

The gentle Henry James; the fat, imperturbable Mark Hanna; the smoldering Frances Willard, the neighborly and engaging Richard Harding Davis—these

move recognizable along a Fifth avenue agleam on rainy
nights with the facets of a hundred glistening hansoms
and aclatter then with the lost music of horsebeats on
asphalt.   You begin the day with the sight of Davis
and Crane munching those crisp, delectable rolls they
used to serve under the striped awning of the old
Vienna Bakery on Broadway opposite Grace Church.
You end it amid the flutter of wit and gossip that would
fill the blue air at Mouquin's if the dandified Clyde
Fitch chanced to be supping there after the play with
the round, pink, odd, unflagging Acton Davies.

Then of course there is Mrs. Astor, who moves
majestical through the pageant of a decade which many
have tried to sum up, but none more successfully than
Beer who speaks of it as a time when the word "ironic"
was used as a reproach.   Of Caroline Astor, Beer makes
this note:

"She liked to laugh, but she made known her surprise
that her son should go to dine with Mark Twain.   She
was an admirer of 'Ouida,' so she must have been
literate, yet, hearing that Miss Alice Duer had begun to
publish poems, she cried: 'But the girl's not at all
plain.'"

This anecdote catches the spirit if not the actual outline of what Mrs. Astor really said.   It was not the
beautiful Miss Duer's first adventures in letters which
puzzled her so much as the tidings that she had decided
to go to Barnard.   With mingled bewilderment and

compassion for poor Mrs. Duer at this news of a daughter's goings on, Mrs. Astor ejaculated:

"Why, she seems such a *nice* girl."

It is interesting to note how loyally Crane's biographer adopts his own antipathies.  The Frances Willard who emerges quite humanized from the recent pages of *Strenuous Americans* is scarcely recognizable there as the same woman who glowers shrewishly in the dark corners of Mr. Beer's book.  As an incongruous undergraduate in the Methodist precincts of Syracuse University, Crane had declined flatly to be introduced to Miss Willard, whom he regarded as a fool because of the "written mayhem" she had committed on the gentle person of Richard Watson Gilder when he let the word "rape" slip into the pages of *The Century*.  And years later Crane was saying:  "I have loved myself passionately now and then, but Miss Willard's affair with Miss Willard should be stopped by the police."

And, on the other hand, note again and again how Davis's stubborn championship of Stephen Crane has kept him princely in the eyes of Crane's biographer—Davis, whom he credits, justly enough, with a chivalry that leaves him "lonely in the tale of American letters."

Perhaps we needed Beer's reminder that Davis's honest and loyal defense of the mud spattered Stanford White led his books to be dumped from a public library in New Jersey, "while lads were warned by the headmaster of a famous school to beware "Soldiers of

Fortune"and "The Princess Aline" as foul emanations of a depraved monster." Indeed, it is a passing reference to the hospitality of Davis's heart that moves Beer to his most blazing sentence: "This oddity of temperament," he says, "got him into trouble when Stanford White was murdered by some inconsequent fellow in a quarrel over a trumpery woman who then was shown at the trial tricked out as a schoolgirl." So much for that.

Indeed, what one hears again and again as this tale moves on is the faint, distant drumbeats of lost causes. One cannot read far without putting down the book from time to time to think how warmly Crane would have been nourished (and surprised) if he could have looked forward and seen such work as "Rain" and the plays of Eugene O'Neill.

It is difficult to believe that it was only thirty years ago that publishers shied at such a fierce and ugly book as Crane's gauche, boyish "Maggie: A Girl of the Streets." And even when a little fame won by "The Red Badge of Courage" smoked out a publisher at last for "Maggie" it was nervously printed. Reading yesterday the 1896 edition of it we came upon the most delicate reservations. Here was a tale of hideous squalor. Jets of violet, fastidious oaths mount to the sky. Yet when the word "hell" or the word "damn" is requisitioned by the author the publisher saves his face by leaving the vowel out of each word. Such apologetic coughing in the midst of a tale is startling now—as startling as it would have been to have had Mr. O'Neill's *Hairy Ape* pause in the midst of his wildest abuse and murmur: "Excuse my wet glove!"

The richer for a little fame and truly loved by a few fine people here and there in the world, Crane died, where Anton Tchekhov did, amid the incomparable beauty of the Black Forest. There is a beer garden there at Badenweiler, where they still tell you how you can find the room upstairs in which Stephen Crane died. If some prophetic soul could have stood at his bedside that last June afternoon and told him that after a score of years his biography would be published in America he would have been a good deal interested, probably.

"Conrad will do it," he would have said hopefully.

"No."

"Then Dick Davis, of course."

"No."

"Who then?"

"Thomas Beer."

"And who might Thomas Beer be?"

"Oh, he's a ten-year-old youngster immured now in a private school at Yonkers."

"Poor kid," Crane would have said with a grin and thought back perhaps to the curbs and lanes and brutes of Whilomville.

# IRVING BERLIN

EACH year now the lovely but ravenous "Music Box" in Forty-fifth Street picks up Irving Berlin by the scruff of his neck, turns him upside down and shakes out of his inexhaustible pockets a very shower of new minted melodies and new wrought rhythms, which, before another year has come, will set the feet of all the world a-tapping. Long after the tinsel and satins of the new revue have gone into the scrap basket, long after the comicalities of Master Tinney and Master Benchley have been overlaid with new humors and forgotten, you will hear the tunes jingling away as gayly or as wistfully as ever. They will drive the wild young drummer at the Hotel Ruhl in Nice to new excesses of contortion; they will be danced to amid the ructions at Moscow, and one of them will float down to you from some wheezy orchestra when next you pace the streets of Shanghai. This prophecy is recorded with conviction (and not without a touch of exasperation) by one who once spent a summer roaming Europe in vain quest of a spot to lay his head where it would *not* be besieged by the strains of "Say It With Music."

As like as not it will be only when you hear these melodies adrift in a strange land that you will know for sure how good they are. The singers and the settings remain on the "Music Box" stage, but the tunes go dancing down the stage door alley and out into the world. Already one of them has come and settled down in our house, for it is impossible to play cribbage —impossible even to say "Fifteen two and a pair is four, fifteen four and a pair is six"—without playing it to the melody of "Climbing Up the Scale." You may like the "California" song even better when you hear it in a grove of which the pendent oranges are *not* electrically luminous and where the lusty young farm hand (unlike John Steel) is not addicted to tight fitting overalls of robin's egg blue velvet. You may really savor the lovely "Bedtime" song when it is not sung by the beauteous and golden Grace Moore sitting pretty in a chair from the wicker rim of which the heads of the disembodied chorus men protrude like unwelcome excrescences to warble the competitive refrain. It is altogether possible that these odd devices enhance the "Music Box" for the yokelry, but somehow amid all its splendors we Olympians are occasionally reminded of that Bad Taste Exhibit in which the first prize went to a Venus de Milo, which was as charming as ever except for the added detail that she had a clock in her stomach.

If we were George Horace Lorimer (admittedly an heroic feat in supposition) we should invite Irving

Berlin to tell the tale of his adventures for the *Saturday Evening Post*. As like as not, at the very suggestion our hero would vanish like a startled rabbit and not be seen hereabouts for many a moon, but it would be worth trying, for there is a thrilling story there to be told some day. It would be a story of a forlorn little Russian immigrant who at the age of four was brought to this country to hide from the cruelty of a land of which he now remembers nothing save the night when the sky was alight with the flames of his own home burning. A story of a hungry, knockabout education in the streets of New York's East Side—the boyhood of a small, thin, big eyed youngster whose first swim came when, as an expression of disapprobation, the Irish boys of the Cherry Hill world dropped him into the East River.

There would be the tale of his first piano, which stood in the sawdust of a dilapidated Bowery hole-in-the-wall, where sailors loose in this port bought drinks for the girls they would leave behind them when the big ships moved on. Berlin's income in those days, considerably smaller than it is now, was pitched at him. It came in pennies from such as these. And then one morning, when the straggling daylight cleared the dive, there was left only the waiter and the boy and the piano, on the battered keys of which Berlin picked out wistfully his first tune. The memories of those days which occasion-ally stray into print are all of the wild times at Nigger

Mike's, where for six years Berlin gathered a little fame as the singing waiter. The black old rascal who was lord of that sinister dive was Berlin's boss until the morning when the boy was found sound asleep by the unguarded till, with his head pillowed on the bar. Here would come tales of burglars rubbing shoulders with sightseeing princes, of tong wars and a song cut short by a knife between the ribs, of vendettas and a calm, contemptuous murder with a man left prone in a suddenly deserted street, spitting out his last blood on the Christmas snow. Indeed, it was from such a saloon as sent *Salvation Nell* into the world that Irving Berlin came up town with his head full of a thousand tunes.

His first job in the theater? Well, that was when Harry Von Tilzer engaged him to plug a new song. Berlin was to haunt the balcony at some vaudeville house—was it Tony Pastor's?—and thence to lift his treble in a song that would be played on the saxophone by Mrs. Keaton, she of the Three Keatons, a variety team which consisted also of a father and of a small boy whom the father at intervals used to hurl against the scenery in a most comical manner. That small missile is not only a famous movie actor now but also a wealthy corporation, the valuable stock of which, they say, is held in no inconsiderable amount by that other boy who sang in the balcony that week.

Then there would be tales, too, of Berlin's first

published song, which he had to compose on the spur of the moment because it was only a verse without a tune when he tried to sell it. Most biographers would linger longest over another song, of which this time it was the lyric that was added suddenly as an afterthought, because a new song was needed that afternoon. That was "Alexander's Ragtime Band," of which the exultant rhythm sent a new lilt adrift in the world and of which, if you dwell on heredity, the melody had begun to brew in Russia generations before. It was written when Berlin was twenty-three.

But if the writer of these fleeting notes were the biographer the climax of the story would not come at "Alexander's Ragtime Band." It would come at another song, which (with the possible exception of " The Battle Hymn of the Republic ") is, to our notion, the best American song. It is as native, as lusty, as amusing and as ornery as " Huckleberry Finn." The song writer called it "Oh, I Hate to Get Up in the Morning." There, for once in a way, was a war song written by a soldier for other soldiers, and you may be sure there were no heroics in it. Somehow "Over There," a really glorious marching tune, was, when coupled with its lyric, a little too reminiscent of the true story of the city editor to whom a naturally alarmed reporter telephoned in that the man he was sent to interview had told him he would put a bullet in the brain of any reporter who so much as rang the doorbell again. "You go back," the editor replied sternly, "you go back and tell that fellow he can't intimidate *me*."

But one militariiy insignificant buck private at Yaphank put into words and music the true thoughts of four million young and inglorious fellow citizens. Do you remember how, to a tune that caught up the usually unwelcome bugle notes, the refrain ran:

> Oh, how I hate to get up in the morning,
> Oh, how I'd love to remain in bed;
> For the hardest blow of all
> Is to hear the bugler call
> > *You've got to get up,*
> > *You've got to get up,*
> > *You've got to get up this morning!*
> Some day I'm going to murder the bugler,
> Some day they're going to find him dead;
> I'll amputate his reveille
> And step upon it heavily
> And spend the rest of my life in bed—
> > *And then I'll get that other pup,*
> > *The one that wakes the bugler up,*
> > *And spend the rest of my life in bed.*

The new show at the "Music Box" is full of good songs, with some of which we expect to wear out the patience of our neighbors this winter, but the reviewer who lazily says that Berlin never wrote any so good before has a quarrel on his hands with several million compatriots who remember what it was to try to wrap a puttee with cold fingers in the dark.

But to return to that projected biography. Back a

little way somewhere the word "thrilling" was affixed to it in advance. Not that Berlin has had hair's-breadth escapes or fled at night down crooked streets with a crazy murderer at his heels. (Not that he hasn't, of course). But his story must be thrilling to those who, glorying as they do in the memory of an age when gallant adventurers wrung a living from this resisting new land, like to be reminded from time to time that, just as in the days when the French explorers sailed wondering down the Mississippi and the boastful Capt. John Smith came up the little James, so now in our own day the romance that is called America is a tale still being told.

Perhaps it might be well to explain at this point that Berlin is a tottering old musician of thirty-six.

# THE MOST STROLLING PLAYER

THIS is a fond piece about the most strolling player of them all. Her name is Elsie Janis. The piece is fond because I do not know her like. There is a little magic in her mimicry. She can tell a story as no one can. And when she dances, the sight is somehow as exhilarating as a cool, fresh wind along an Alpine road in May. But then the piece is fond, too, because, by chance, I have crossed her path so often and so unexpectedly. All this is set down by one who has run into her in odd places like Windsor and Vincennes and Philadelphia. And I have a vague notion that everywhere I have ever been, she was either there or had just been there. In a single year, the first three performances of hers of which I heard tell were on a boat in the Mediterranean, on a platform at the Sorbonne (where the students awarded her a medal they had given in all time to only two other actresses) and in the great hall at Sing Sing. I think that last was the one which *she* enjoyed.

The Broadwayites who observed one week that the name of Elsie Janis had moved out of its old stamping ground in the theatrical columns to reappear suddenly and unexpectedly in the sedater areas devoted to concert announcements were probably a trifle bewildered by that phenomenon. Here was a comedienne who could, with much less effort, go dancing into vaudeville whenever she felt like it and emerge staggering under purses of gold. Or who could, if she wished, step into any of the great revues and shine there as she shone when "The Century Girl" was loose on the stage where recently Duse and Martin Harvey, by turns, were classically engaged. Yet here she was taking willfully to the byways of concert. Why?

Well, one who these many years has kept an often startled but always affectionate eye on the roving Miss Janis can only hazard a guess. A guess that she wished, long before advancing years would compel her to abandon the gay steps and exuberant cartwheels of her music hall tricks and manners, to establish for future use the fact that she could be just such a diseuse as was the Yvette Guilbert of the long black gloves, who first passed majestically this way when Little Elsie was giving entertainments in the church back home in Columbus. A guess, too, that the days of her wild barnstorming in the A. E. F. (when she needed only her mother as stage manager, property man, wardrobe mistress and supporting cast) bred in her an unquenchable preference for being her own impresario or having none. And that she would hesitate to sign any contract for a long engagement here, knowing full well what a deep nostalgia would possess her when the first green shoots in Central Park reminded her that spring was thrilling, too, along the Champs Elysées. And stirring a hubbub of new life in that garden on the Thames at Datchett, where she has an annual engagement to feed two swans, who, to the considerable amusement of any one that has ever shopped in Piccadilly, answer to the names of Swann and Edgar respectively.

When first I went to London that phlegmatic town was talking of nothing but the frightfully clever American girl who had been singing "Florrie Was a Flapper" at the Palace. I lived to hear Frenchmen exhausting their shoulders in an effort adequately to give some notion of their sentiments about "*la grande vedette Americaine*"—and to rock with laughter at their expressions while, in a Gallo-African style of her own, she sang them "*Moi, j'ai un béguin pour' Arry.*"

Once I saw her having the time of her life watching stray riffraff at the *Lapin Agile* on Montmartre, and feeling apparently that she was just an unrecognizable part of that dear Paris, when, as one after another of the patrons volunteered a song, suddenly a gruff, unmistakable American voice issued unexpectedly from beneath a French student's cap with the suggestion, "Say, Elsie, sing 'em 'Smiles.'"

That was just a bit of the A. E. F. still stranded in Paris, to whom the sight of her recalled a day in the rain when a lean American girl in a short skirt and a jaunty tam stood on a roadside truck and sang to 10,000 soldiers—sang till a still, small voice became so very still and so very small that she couldn't hear it herself. There were other show folk who gave themselves as freely and as fully as Elsie Janis did. There was that grand old vaudeville team of Cressy and Dane, for instance. But there was none who outdid her.

She is probably the only American in our theater who can play in London and Paris (and could play in Berlin) without afflicting the natives. Except for certain of the movie folk, who, like Mr. Chaplin and Miss Pickford, can tour by parcel post, she is probably better known abroad than any of our players. It seems doubtful if any such outcome was forecast by any of the fond prophets who beamed upon her in the days when she was Elsie Bierbauer of Columbus, *la petite vedette Ohian*, so ardently given to imitating her minister and her postman and her cook and her dog, that at the very sight of a church spire she must have instinctively started for the Sunday school platform, just hot to recite.

She had reached the maturer age of five or thereabouts before she actually went on the professional stage—playing occasional children's rôles, not only with the stock company in Columbus but in Cincinnati as well, where, to this day, one of the critics so vividly recalls her first performance that every time she plays his town he can't resist telling how long ago it was.

Of course she played "Little Lord Fauntleroy," as who did not? Indeed, that item is set down here in the hope of inciting some patient annalist to draw up a chart of all the *Little Lord Fauntleroys* such as Master Wallace Eddinger and dear little Eva Tanguay, for instance, who were allowed to live on.

She was billed at first as Little Elsie, and at one period an enterprising management further proclaimed in the programs that she was, as some reviewer had said, a pocket edition of Cissie Loftus—the same Cissie Loftus who, in the whirligig of time was to include the now lanky little Elsie in her own repertoire of imitations. It was Rockwood, the photographer of children, who, when her lengthening legs began to take issue with the name Little Elsie, told her that Elsie Bierbauer would never look well on the ash cans. And it was Rockwood who, after hearing unmoved all the patronymics in her family tree, pounced delightedly on Janis, the given name of her French grandmother.

The more exciting adventures of Little Elsie in those days, when she played always under the unflagging management of her mother, consisted of affectedly nonchalant appearances in New York, made uneasy by the suspicion that the Gerry Society would chase her out, as invariably it did. There is a legend that stage children are simply forbidden by their mercenary parents to grow up. It is a legend based on the *Infant Phenomenon* of "Nicholas Nickleby," who remained precisely 10 years old for a good five years, and who, by being kept up late every night and being put on a unlimited allowance of gin and water from infancy, was prevented from growing tall. This legend, which doubtless accounts to some extent for the preposterous raids on stage children that benevolent outsiders are forever instigating, runs counter to most experience. Like Minnie Maddern before her—Minnie Maddern, who brazened it out as the *Widow Melnotte* when she was only 13—Elsie Janis appears to have panted with impatience to grow up, and she was an old timer of 15 when she finally began her first undisturbed New York engagement in "The Vanderbilt Cup."

From the first she had the gift which she still has— that of uncanny and critical mimicry. It is a fine art in itself, and yet, when it is given in full measure to one like Miss Janis and Miss Loftus, it is invariably and perversely accompanied by an inner itch not to be a mimic at all. Elsie Janis began these travesties of hers when she was all curls and pink silk dresses in the churches of Columbus. Thus it befell one night that when she was working overtime in a smoky Y hut in France and asked the troops what imitations they wanted, there came from a ferocious old mess sergeant down front a hoarse demand for Dan Daly. She blushed and started to murmur shyly that she was much too young to remember Dan Daly, but these pretty protestations were cut short by the mess sergeant who roared severely: "I seen you imitate Dan Daly when you was knee high to a grasshopper."

Some of her most extraordinary imitations are of French players who are unknown here. And those who have never watched her at work in a hall so small that the finest shading can be seen do not know at all how startlingly real and delicate and true are some of her reproductions. For instance, she has never used an imitation of John Barrymore in any of her programs, and yet she can so catch his very voice and expression and gesture that the next time he is called suddenly abroad in the middle of a performance of "Hamlet" there will be no real necessity of ringing down the curtain.

All of which rambling remarks about one of the most entertaining members of the human race seem, as I look back over them, to be cast in such a vein of doddering reminiscence that one could hardly blame the careless reader who found himself thinking of Elsie Janis and Eleanora Duse as just two contemporaneous girls trying to get along. When once informed that the former was born in 1890 all those equipped with pencil, paper and a knack of arithmetic will know the worst.

# JOHN DREW

It was fifty years ago and more that a jaunty, twinkling young fellow named John Drew made his first appearance on the stage. This début took place at the famous theater over which his mother presided in Arch Street, Philadelphia—now a forlorn and dilapidated playhouse left behind in a mean thoroughfare. I remember it in my own school days as a cheap burlesque house with tatters of gaudy posters fluttering from its sickly yellow front and, precious and fastidious even then, I passed it by, nose in air, on my way to what the natives called Keith's Buyjoe around the corner in Eighth Street. But fifty years ago it was the commanding theater of its city. A city where the Drews were already such established traditions that all the audience shared and enjoyed the joke when Mrs. Drew, gazing quizzically at the neophyte, interpolated this line. "What a dreadful young man! I wonder what he will be like when he grows up?" A city of such long memories that, a generation later, when this same Mrs. Drew's granddaughter made her nervous, half choked first appearance there in "Captain Jinks," a fond voice in the gallery called down: "Speak up, Ethel. You're all right. The Drews is all good actors."

In the meantime the dreadful young man aforesaid may be said to have grown up, and one night in the spring of 1923 at the Biltmore that fiftieth anniversary was fittingly observed with feasting and high or medium jinks. It was a dinner in honor of the adroit and unfailing comedian of whom Booth Tarkington had said that he would make *Simon Legree* a misunderstood gentleman. It was a dinner in honor of one who to a rare degree had commanded (and probably enjoyed) the respect of his countrymen and the boundless affection of his fellow players the world around. As one who, sharing that respect and that affection, would have liked to join in the celebrations I was minded to assemble, if possible, a small company of his peers and, taking a table for them just as the 1909 men do at a college dinner, lead, let us say, Mr. Sothern, Mr. Gillette and Mrs. Fiske in several long cheers, ending with three John Drews and a Bravo. But that would have involved attending a banquet which, after a recent depressing experience, I had resolved should never happen again.

Then it seemed a good notion to escort these three players to Mr. Drew's quarters on the anniversary morn as a deputation loaded down with good will. But the getting them together seemed likely to be a game as exasperating as Pigs in Clover, and anyway the sudden memory of a painful incident disconcerted me. It was during the famous actors' strike, when the bewildered managers, feeling the tide of popular feeling running unaccountably against them, felt that it was probably the fault of the newspapers and that something more sympathetic might be injected into the daily accounts if a sufficiently imposing and formidable delegation were to make the rounds of the managing editors. Thus one evening just such a delegation of four bore down on the small urchin guarding the anteroom of the New York *Times* and expressed a willingness to confer with the managing editor.

"Will you be good enough to tell him," said one, "that Mr. David Belasco, Mr. George Broadhurst, Mr. E. H. Sothern and Mr. Harrison Grey Fiske wish to see him?"

"All four of you?" cried the boy aghast.

"Yes, my lad, all four of us."

"What do you want to do? Sing to him?"

So it seemed best just to suggest that the message of good will be set forth in print instead. It was Mr. Sothern who spoke first:

"Of course, I, in common with all actors, must rejoice that Mr. Drew, after fifty years of honorable service, is to receive from the community so well deserved a tribute. It is something to have stood all these years for what is best and most wholesome in the theater, and

in complimenting Mr. Drew people are confessing the
good taste of our theatergoers whose approval has
enabled Mr. Drew to prevail for half a century.  Per-
sonally, I wish him joy 'of the occasion,' which will be
delightful and replete with affectionate remembrances.

"I hope that Mr. Drew will not announce his retirement.  This announcement is a weakness to which we
are prone, and which, when the glamour and the tears
befitting the occasion have been properly admired and
shed, we are apt to regret, or to feel that the tax gatherer
should previously have been consulted.  Mr. Drew being still young, such a catastrophe as his retirement
must not be considered.  Through you may I wish him
good fortune and godspeed?"

Then listen to one who, for this occasion, fell neatly into the grand manner of the old comedies.

"I am but one of the thousands of human atoms that
wish to felicitate John Drew—First Gentleman of the
American Stage—upon the occasion of his golden jubilee
as an actor, and to express gratitude for the pleasure
and happiness that his splendid art and admirable personality have contributed to the mimic world.  A true
aristocrat of the theater, he has always more than
fulfilled his obligations to his heritage and sustained
those alluring, elegant and refining phases of the player's art that, but for him and a few like him, would have

perished from the scene. Continued happiness to him and the warm, affectionate hope that he may long continue to delight us with his ripe art and be an exemplar to his younger colleagues of everything that they should aspire to be, for doubtless we shall never see his like again.

"MINNIE MADDERN FISKE."

The next witness called was William Gillette. He took the stand protesting hotly that not a word of testimony would he give.

"Allow me the privilege of remonstrating with you," wrote Mr. Gillette. "Suppose, as the 'ten to a thousand words' of greeting to John Drew is for your theater page in the *Herald*, and not for him, that you write it. I am much fonder of 'Uncle John' than you could possibly be, but he does not care two damns about being 'greeted' by me. Indeed I am inclined to think it would annoy him very much. But if *your* page needs it that is another matter. Anything I can do for *you*—except writing it—shall be done. You plunge ahead *ad lib.* (as we say in play manuscripts when we nurse the hope that the actor will be able to help us along a bit) and write anything you like and I will sign it before a notary and two witnesses. But I won't write it myself unless the *Herald* takes me on its staff."

I should have liked to serve, too, as messenger boy for

one nosegay that went to the Biltmore that night. It was a handful of rosemary. Said the card that went with it: "This is for remembrance, dear Uncle Jasper." The card was unsigned, but Mr. Drew must have known that it could have come from only one person in all the world—Maude Adams.

Yes, as the gallery god so justly observed when "Captain Jinks" was tried out at the old Walnut Street Theater, the Drews *is* all good actors, and this dinner was to one of a great line. Its festivity was merely one chapter in the history of a remarkable tradition, this dinner to one who, as a youngster underfoot in Philadelphia, heard his mother and his grandmother reminiscing of performances given down the Mississippi in the second decade of the nineteenth century and of great occasions in the theater in the America the young Charles Dickens visited. A player, Mr. Drew, like his mother and his father before him, like his grandmother and his grandfather before *them*. The tale is still being told. That first performance fifty years ago was a benefit for Georgie Drew, whose children, the three Barrymores, are writing new chapters in the record each season. And on the first night of "Romeo and Juliet" at the Longacre that winter the performance was watched by another Ethel Barrymore, wide eyed, pretty and ten years old, whose own appearance as *Juliet* I confidently expect to review one of these days.

And if you want to savor an impalpable quality

which has invested Mr. Drew's performances through the years, which has entered into the inevitable choice of him as president of the Players and which lies far back of the good will which that dinner tried to express, consider as a clew the letter printed on the thirteenth page of "My Years on the Stage," the book of Mr. Drew's memories published by Dutton. The letter was written from Philadelphia on November 12, 1863, by Mrs. Drew at a time when "the dreadful young man" was a youngster at a military school in Village Green. It reads thus:

"MY DEAR SON—I received yours of the 9th inst. to-day. To-morrow will be your birthday, my darling —you are ten years old to-morrow. All your family wish you many, many happy returns of the day. I can't send you any birthday present, as you are so soon to come home. Sorry that the shoes are too large, but if you can get along till you come home I will get you a pair to fit better. Of course, you can take your sledge back with you. Take good care of yourself, and as it is cold early in the morning don't waste time in dressing yourself. All send love. God bless you, dear. Your affectionate mother,

"LOUISA DREW."

So the dinner was to one who, after a life spent in the most vagrant of callings and nearly a half century in a

city that remembers nothing and has no attics, nevertheless had with him when, coming on toward seventy,
he sat down to write out the print of his remembrance,
the little letter his mother wrote him the night before he
was ten years old.

# MORRIS GEST

IT was in 1898 that Constantin Stanislavsky opened the Moscow Art Theater. In all the depiction of emotion his players have undertaken since then we doubt if any have equaled the amused incredulity that would have flashed from the face of that lofty and zealous amateur had some prophet come to him on the first night and told him that twenty-five years later, in the whirligig of time, his troupe would be summoned to America and sponsored there by one who was then a half-starved fifteen-year-old waif in Boston, a runaway Jew from Russia, who had given up the unexciting business of selling newspapers along Pi Alley and gone in as handy man around a Yiddish theater which had drifted up from New York.

Judging from the prospecting that certain magazine editors and book publishers have been up to lately it seems reasonably certain that a biography of Morris Gest will look down from the shelf before long. If it tells half the truth it will be a lively and entertaining and, in some ways, an exhilarating tale. Such a book would probably have a chapter about a turbulent childhood in Russia. It would show an undisciplined, hobbledehoy boy so frequently larruped and cast into a rat-ridden cellar by a stern and distrustful father that both of them were relieved when the son decided he would rather try his luck in the remote and fabulous land called America. It will sketch in the great-grandfather a bearded, crinkle-faced patriarch, who, in bidding the young emigrant farewell, held forth for the purpose a skinny hand, of which all but two fingers had been paralyzed, but of which the force in those two was so great that Gest can still feel the pressure of them as they were laid on his head in a gloomy benediction.

The book will have a record of the first haphazard adventures as a showman, the first ingenious essays in the business of hornswoggling the public. A boy taking tickets at a burlesque house and then going back stage to lie on his back under the ground cloth and kick in a maritime manner for the shipwreck scene. A boy making his contribution to his new country's war against Spain by organizing the first Hobson Kiss Ball —quaintly enough at Puritan Hall in Boston. A boy adrift among the county fairs up Buzzards Bay and Old Orchard and Portland way, now cleaning the monkey cage in Bostock's circus, now helping a dilapidated medicine man sell soap, now busy catching sparrows and painting them yellow for the canary trade. Surely a hint of the future lay in the great day when he enlisted as aid to a forlorn fellow who had one of these new fangled phonographs with rubber tubes and ear pieces by which the passing bumpkins, on paying each a penny, could hear the raucous tunes. To whip up trade the young assistant announced "The Ravings of John McCullough," after first, with much shrieking and horrible moaning, having made the record himself.

It was Sam H. Harris, as manager for Terry McGovern in "The Road to Ruin," who first brought Gest to New York, but the chapter of that period will have to be devoted rather to Oscar Hammerstein, who sold to the young newcomer the ticket speculator privilege of the lobby in the then wabbly and impecunious Victoria, a shoddy variety theater where they were less happy in booking the best clown of the day than in engaging for one week or one fortnight the girl who had committed the most gaudy murder then occupying the front pages of the newspapers. It was Gest who was sent to Europe to buy up attractions for the Victoria and who came back proudly with a German household, a stolid Berliner with his wife, sister-in-law and daughter, whom Gest bedecked in Moslem costumes, instructed to pray ostentatiously to the East every day at sunset on the boat coming over, and covered with fleeting fame by having them rejected at a Broadway hotel, where they had tried to register as Abdul Kaffir and wives. That delighted German still has land at Atlantic City which he bought with the profits of that little tour. Probably the chapter on Hammerstein will close with the glory of the first night at the new Manhattan. It will tell how, on the very afternoon of the day the defiant impresario was to open his rival to the nervous Metropolitan, the new opera house had not yet been cleaned out, and how Gest, getting hold of fifty brooms, went out on the streets and organized from the home going schoolboys a troupe of cleaners who would help him sweep it out. So the old legend is true that Gest himself swept out the opera house which he was one day to buy, and it is probable that the grime of that exploit was still on him that night, when, after the falling of the final curtain, he and Hammerstein trotted off alone to Childs' in Thirty-fourth Street and sat for hours together planning the future of opera in America.

There will, of course, be a chapter on Gest's hero— David Belasco. The story will begin with the riotous success of Mrs. Leslie Carter in "Du Barry" at what is now called the Republic Theater; of how Gest, by spending all his days in the ticket line, used to accumulate enough of stray seats to make a neat profit on the sidewalk, and of how Belasco himself gradually became aware that this wild but distinctly reverent looking young Russian was always sitting on the doorstep of the theater when, even at four or five o'clock in the morning, he himself would be starting home. Just as Gest always managed to turn up last winter in any town where Chaliapin happened to be singing, so you would always see him in Syracuse or Baltimore if by any chance a new Belasco production was being tried out there.  It happened one night that a supper party was given at Childs' restaurant in New Haven to the company of "The Grand Army Man," the Warfield play which had opened there that evening.  Just as the party was sitting down it was discovered in a panic that it numbered thirteen, and Acton Davies went scurrying around to find an eleventh hour guest to take the curse off.  Inevitably his eyes lighted on the wistful Gest, who was sitting in a corner letting a campanile of wheat cakes grow cold upon his plate.  It was at that supper that the young Russian met Belasco's daughter, who is now Mrs. Gest.

The story will tell of his passion for mere color, which intoxicates him and which he craves as other men crave whisky.  We saw him once at the Savoy in London on the night when Liberty's agents had delivered to him a hamper of old robes, prayer rugs and the like specially garnered for him from among the bazaars in India. We have an unforgettable picture of him trying with scant success at three in the morning to infuse into Heifetz (who wanted to eat) and Herbert Kauffman (who wanted to talk about the international oil situation) something of his own Levantine enthusiasm for the glories in blue and green and crimson that had come to him out of the magical East.  For himself he was a cat with catnip.  That picture is the necessary key to his grandiose productions of "Chu Chin Chow," "Aphrodite" and "Mecca," adventures in the theater, now profitable, now disastrous, which the book must cover. But the book will have missed the point if it does not suggest how, in the long run, the theater will take care of itself. Just as the little manager from the East Side who toured the country with Terry McGovern in "The Road to Ruin" became sponsor now of the playhouse where the foremost *Hamlet* of its generation was first revealed, just as the Minnie Maddern, who came to town in 1882 as a red headed soubrette in an incredible piece of balderdash called "Fogg's Ferry," was later to return to it in "Rosmersholm" and "Hedda Gabler," so in time the theater was to take that young man who painted the sparrows yellow years ago in Maine and do something to him, which would make him more eager and proud to have his name on the program of Stanislavsky's company, on the playbills of Reinhardt's first venture in America and on those of Duse's farewell tour, than to own outright the most successful piece of ordinary, undistinguished hokum now raking in the profits anywhere in the world.

# OUR BETTERS

IT was in an infrequent moment of graciousness that your correspondent permitted himself to drop in for a few moments one Spring afternoon at the Cort Theater, where the boys and girls from the Professional Children's School were gravely engaged in their own production of "Merton of the Movies." The visit was that of a busy critic who, it might as well be admitted now in sackcloth and ashes, was in the condescending mood of those insufferable adults that have the effrontery to call a child a "tot" or a "kiddie."

The intention was to stay for a scene and slip away, strong in the consciousness of duty done and courtesy rendered. Well, we never did begrudge a final curtain so fervently. And all other engagements for the afternoon of April 26th were thereby canceled. For the junior "Merton" was to be repeated then and one no more misses such things than one forgets to use the Metropolitan seats when Chaliapin is singing *Boris*.

The business in hand then was to get the word around town to the playgoers who would especially enjoy this entertainment, for it seemed a pity to let the seats for the second performance get into the hands of those to whom it would be only a rather amusing pastime.

The man at the box office should have put each applicant for tickets through a sort of quiz and, just as a suggestion, this was offered as a good test question: "When you used to go to 'Peter Pan' and the dimming of the lights spread a bated hush over the jabber of the auditorium and the tiny *Liza* with fearful solemnity used to come before the curtain and stamp for the orchestra to strike up, did you suddenly feel an absurd and inexplicable lump in your throat? What? You didn't? Sorry then, but we're all sold out."

We immediately became busy with plans for our own box party on that occasion. We wanted seats for Mrs. Fiske, Maude Adams, Booth Tarkington, Kate Douglas Wiggin and Sir James M. Barrie. Two vacant seats were held until the final curtain because of a persistent notion that somehow those for whom they were intended would manage to attend a performance they were so especially equipped to enjoy. Thus there was a seat for Eugene Field and another for Charles Dickens.

The performance was organized by Billy Janney. He is the son of the Russell Janney, who had been instrumental the year before in the production of "Marjolaine." Janney, *fils*, was then twelve years old and since the beginnings of "Merton" he has been playing the part of the kid who stands by the disillusioned Galahad from Simsbury on the night of his great ordeal.

During all these months he had been watching Glenn Hunter, wide eyed, sopping Hunter up as a new blotting paper takes ink. Now there was not a toss of the Hunter head, a pucker of the Hunter eyebrows, a tone of the Hunter voice, that he could not reproduce in miniature. He even managed to stand all out of drawing as only Hunter and Airedale terriers could do. It was as uncanny a feat in reproduction as Elsie Janis can manage only when the subject is one she knows by heart.

So of course it was Billy Janney who played *Merton Gill*. The whole company was clever, spirited and immensely engaging, from the pretty Vivian Tobinesque girl named Natalie Browning, who was the *Montague girl*, to the morsel of a violinist who played in the rehearsal scene, a small lamb of God who did his part with a gravity that was overwhelming.

They were all good but, after all, it was Billy Janney's afternoon. We suspect it was a pretty tired, flushed and happy young actor who tried hard to get to sleep that night but who must have been a little dolorous in reflecting on the interminable stretch of years before he would be twenty-one and could do "bigger and finer" things, like *Hamlet*. Bless us all, in no time he will be wondering where those years have gone to and wondering if the critics will say he is too old for some part he had always itched to play.

They say it had been eleven years since the last of
these junior performances was given. That was when
"Disraeli" in little was done down at the since
obliterated Wallack's, and one of the minor maidens of
the cast was a fragment of an actress named Genevieve
Tobin. Just before that were the children's casts of
"Pomander Walk" and "Alias Jimmy Valentine," the
latter with Warner's rôle played by Donald Gallaher.
It is an old custom of the theater and if that box party
had been arranged, Mrs. Fiske could have told us
between the acts about the time when in just such a
company she played *Ralph Rackstraw* for a hundred
performances of "Pinafore," and Miss Marlowe, if she
had been in town, could have told of the prodigious
occasion when she played *Uncle Tom*.

Children of the theater Mrs. Fiske and Miss Marlowe
were—just such children as these who had the time
of their lives that happy afternoon at the Cort, just such
children as arouse the fatuous interventionists who, especially in other communities, are continuously blunder-
ing conscientiously into the theater and dragging them
away to less sheltering, less nourishing and less pro-
ductive lives.

All the young fry engaged in the junior "Merton"
were wage earners at an age when most of us are loafers.
All of them were actors. The likes of them must have a
school of their own, one which can adjust its schedule of
classes to fit the hours of children thus launched early in

the world that is to make them and which they are to remake as it has been eternally remade since the beginning.   This school is at 312 West Seventy-second Street.   It was Billy Janney, a pupil there, who, out of his own excitement, generated sufficient enthusiasm to propel his elders toward a performance that some of us enjoyed beyond words to tell.

# THE LETTER OF MONSIEUR AIMÉ

IN Baldridge's celebrated painting called "November Eleventh," one sees two rangy young Westerners, their guns and gas masks dropped at their sides, standing up in a shallow Flanders trench, gazing into space. Some there are who would tell you that each of them, in his vision, saw a world made free. But others know that these two were merely looking across six thousand miles of land and sea at an unimportant home somewhere in Idaho.

Since the armistice was signed five years ago so many men have risen to point out that it ended a fight which need never have been. Or that it began, rather than ended, the fight. Small wonder that most of us have forgotten what welcome news it was at the time—what jubilant tidings to the millions of ordinary men who had begun to believe they would never see their folks again on this earth. If it was so with the Americans, most of whom had not been in France a single year, how much more was it true of those little French soldiers whose families waited for them on the other side of the line?

Think what it meant to M. Aimé, the small, hairy

café proprietor of Longwy, who, at forty-eight, got out the old uniform when the war began and who, when he was automatically demobilized two years later, found the path blocked that led to home.   It was less than one hundred miles away, but between him and his own front gate stood one million Germans armed to the teeth.   So, to be as near as possible and ready to start up the road whenever the guns should cease firing he got him a job as *gerant* of the café in the Grand Hôtel du Metz et du Commerce at Bar-le-Duc.   There he waited two years, forced to be content with a single message of five words that had come through the Red Cross in Switzerland one Christmas.   That message had said his wife and child were doing well, but had been too official to point out something else Aimé rather wanted to know. Was it a boy or a girl?   It was to have been born in November, 1914.   Aimé did not know whether he had a son or a daughter.

The hotel was a bleak, cheerless old hostelry which stood (and still stands) on the main street of Bar-le-Duc, and it knew lean days in the war until, because Foch had decided that the Americans should throw all their strength into the line between Verdun and the Argonne, the streets of its town in late September, 1918, became thronged overnight with O. D. uniforms.   Through the gates and out again hundreds of thousands of jostling Yankees trudged on their way to the front, headquarters of every description camped out in its battered buildings

and the café of the Metz became so crowded every hour
that Aimé grew almost intolerably busy, self-important
and autocratic. Gaudy American Generals learned at
last what it was to beg for a cup of coffee and then wait
an hour to get it.

But there was one negligible and bespectacled Sergeant for whom, somehow, there was always a place,
always a hot cup and sometimes even a dab of confiture
for the rocky bread. It was among his duties to report
back one day each week to the American press headquarters across the canal and, coming fresh from there,
where he had just read the wireless bulletins from all
fronts, he could, in his ugly but practical French, tell
little Aimé the news for which he was on tiptoe. So
they became fast friends and it was to him that Aimé
turned later in his bewilderment.

That bewilderment followed two days after the firing
of the last shot. The first morning, the bleary eyed
patrons of the Metz café had found it closed, with a sign
on the window telling that the *gerant* had left town forever. But the next day he was back again, anguished
with the tidings that he had been halted on his way
home. In those first days there was such a rush of the
homesick prisoners back to France that the roads were
black and clogged with a tattered, eager rabble and
whole American regiments went hungry while their
kitchens opened up on the roadside to feed these still
hungrier strangers. It was then that the order went out

at least to halt all civilians trying to move toward the frontier and, caught in the claws of this order, poor Aimé had been turned back.

It was when he learned that the American forces would soon be moving forward and that his friend, the Sergeant, would be in the procession that Aimé's hopes were revived. Might the Sergeant be going through Longwy? And would he take a letter? It would be for Mme. Aimé. He could so easily find her—there at the café, a much handsomer café than this one, Monsieur, with red plush seats and mirrors and all. Would he take the letter? Of course he would.

So up went the shutters of the Metz again, and discouraged patrons peering through the chinks all next day could see only the anxious and agitated shoulders of the *gerant* as he bent over white paper with an unaccustomed pen held fiercely in his hand. The letter, page after page of love and longing, was buttoned safe in the courier pocket of the sergeant's blouse when, at noon three days later, after trundling the long road through Verdun and Stenay toward Luxembourg, he quite inexcusably made a detour toward Longwy. It was travel not at all necessary in the military service.

The first sight of the town was dismaying, for not a house was standing, but the sergeant soon discovered that the guns had swept only the hilltop section, and that down in the valley the older village by the church was still there—bullet ridden, disconsolate and dirty, but standing just the same. The café itself was standing, but what made the messenger anxious was the obvious fact that it was, and long had been, deserted, with old boards where its windows had been and within mere ruin, where once all had been red plush and mirrors. Passersby did not know where Mme. Aimé was. Oh, yes, the café was closed. The patronne, it seemed, had refused to serve drinks to the German officers, and the place had been deserted from the first.

The sergeant pushed on with his inquiries. Surely some one must know whither Mme. Aimé had betaken herself. He would ask neighbors, he thought, and on that errand he plodded up a flight of steps and made for the first open door. It opened from a kitchen, where a tall, handsome woman of thirty-five or thereabouts was making bread, while a curly headed, sparkling morsel of a four-year-old maiden was busy beside her, earnestly patting dough into cookies. The sergeant halted in the doorway, pushed the door a little to make room for his own shoulders and started to ask:

"Can you tell me, Madame, where——"

But the opening door gave a view of the living room beyond and there, on its wall, enlarged, horrible, gilt framed and unmistakable, was a beaming photograph of the little man who was waiting back there at the café in Bar-le-Duc. So the sergeant simply handed the letter over in silence. It was the first word from or about her husband that she had had since she had seen him go down the street in his uniform one August morning four years before. While she read the letter the foolish sergeant had to retreat to the hall and look out of the window.

After the excitement had subsided he was hauled back again, and was not suffered to go on his way until he had told all he knew and, with Aimé's enchanting daughter encamped on his knee, he had drawn up to the kitchen table and tackled a bowl of coffee. To his embarrassment, he could see that the mother, who had already blessed him with a smile he would never forget, would not be really content until she had made him some tangible, portable gift and when he finally was started on his way he was the richer by something that she had been hoarding for months and which to her was as a handful of diamonds. Her gift was two pounds of lump sugar.

# AN OPEN LETTER TO A LADY

ANY WELL REGULATED HOME,
December 24, ANY YEAR.

DEAR MAUDE ADAMS:

This is just a line to carry the season's greetings and to tell a little of how much we all miss you. Here it is Christmas Eve. As our old friend *Captain Hook* observed on a celebrated occasion, "I should be feeling deevy, yet over me broods a disky spirit, premonition of impending doom, embracing me inexorably like a closing umbrella." To-morrow the land may be snow mantled and all the frosty air above it atingle and gay with chimes and sleigh bells. Yet there will come no sound from that abandoned creature, *Tinker Bell*, nor all her tribe that used to riot in the treetops at sundown.

It is such a long time since *Peter Pan* waved good-by from his front doorstep in those treetops. It is such a long time since the self-important *Liza* last stamped her foot for the music to begin, since the lost children built the house for *Wendy*, since *Nibs* danced the pillow dance and *Michael*, after slaying a pirate or two, wiped off his

175

cutlass and exclaimed: "I like it, *Wendy*, I like it very much."

Of course you must not think there are no good things on the stage this year. Indeed, there are probably more things that are fine and bold and aspiring than ever before. But I would steal a line from that love letter the enamored bobby wrote to his *Cinderella* from the police station. "There are thirty-four policemen sitting in this room, but I'd rather have you, my dear."

Well, Miss Adams, a Merry Christmas to you. A Merry Christmas and a Happy New Year. I send you my love.

Your fond, multitudinous friend,<br>
THE AMERICAN PLAYGOER.

# II
# RESENTMENTS

# IN 1944

THE book by Kenneth Macgowan called "The Theater of To-morrow" proved thoroughly readable once I was under way, but I found it almost impossible to begin. Perhaps a certain part of the reluctance could be traced by a neurologist to its illustrations, which are superb reproductions in color of dreams that artists have dreamed as to how this scene or that might take form and color on the stage. These pictures nourish a suspicion that in the "Theater of To-morrow," as fore-shadowed in Mr. Macgowan's prophetic soul, there will be more and more miracles of light and line and atmosphere, with the dramatist reduced to playing chorus or merely prompter to the scenery and the actor finally abolished for good and all as a public nuisance.

Or perhaps that reluctance, if not more simply ascribed to gnawing envy of so much learning, might be followed back to an origin in our own dark suspicion that the "Theater of To-morrow" will, after all, bear a certain haunting resemblance to the Theater of To-day. Being of little faith, we suspected that in it each season would witness the following:

1. Eighteen comedies in which the leading actor or actress, having, at some time previous, taken a flier in motion pictures, will be heralded as now making his or her "return to the spoken drama."

2. Twelve revivals of "Twelfth Night" with one restriction in common—that the actress playing the sweet salvage of the Illyrian shore should, under no circumstances, be less than forty-five years old.

3. One hundred and forty-seven plays in which the central feminine character shall be living or (at some time previous) shall have lived, in sin.

4. Twenty-six comedies translated from the French and containing some such racy idiom as this: "It is not that it is necessary that one should go, Mussoor."

5. Forty plays in which the moral and physical disasters which overtake the protagonist are triumphantly corrected by the process of a long final scene in the country, played against a lovely canvas meadow.

6. Fourteen scenes in which mother love is expressed by embracing the progeny and gazing with extreme anguish (and some discomfort to the neck) at a spot in the ceiling immediately overhead. This is known as the Chandelier School of Acting.

7. Sixteen insoluble mystery plays in which the chief crook will turn out in the last act to be either a Central Office detective, a Secret Service operative or a local Sheriff.

8. One hundred plays containing two or more of the following speeches.

"I wonder why I am telling all this to you."

"You mean?"

"Won't you sit down?"

"My God! What a beast I am!"

"Shure'n it's no trouble at all, at all."

"You here?"

9. Seventeen comedies about a little stranger from Shanghai or Madagascar or Bucharest who, being an innocent in the ways of our tongue, will, before the middle of the second act, have said either "hell" or "damn" and probably both, at which utterances all the native characters will gasp, drop dying and fall off furniture by way of deftly expressing mingled astonishment and horror at such unheard of language.

10. Seventy-eight plays in which all dialogues will be spoken with the two actors standing in the middle of an enormous room with their respective noses tickling each other. This is known as the Carbonic School of Acting.

11. Ninety-four plays in which the leading juvenile will make a special point of pronouncing blue as though it were spelled "blee-you."

12. Eleven romances in which the central figure, such as a cowboy or a toreador or a bandit, is described by all the feminine characters as a wild, hot-blooded, splendid young animal, and is played by an actor going on sixty-five.

After which pensive prophecies, it was natural to grow speculative as to who, among all the young players the critics had been loudly discovering, would be reigning *vignt ans après*. Who would be the Mrs. Fiskes and the Ethel Barrymores of 1944? Who would be the Belasco? And where, one wondered, would the theaters themselves be found? This vein of reflection could find outlet only in a glimpse at the theatrical advertisements in any New York newspaper for December 20, 1944. As for instance:

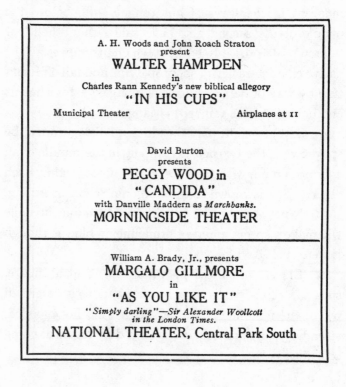

A. H. Woods and John Roach Straton
present
**WALTER HAMPDEN**
in
Charles Rann Kennedy's new biblical allegory
**"IN HIS CUPS"**
Municipal Theater                    Airplanes at 11

David Burton
presents
**PEGGY WOOD in**
**" CANDIDA "**
with Danville Maddern as *Marchbanks.*
**MORNINGSIDE THEATER**

William A. Brady, Jr., presents
**MARGALO GILLMORE**
in
**"AS YOU LIKE IT "**
*" Simply darling "—Sir Alexander Woollcott*
*in the London Times.*
**NATIONAL THEATER, Central Park South**

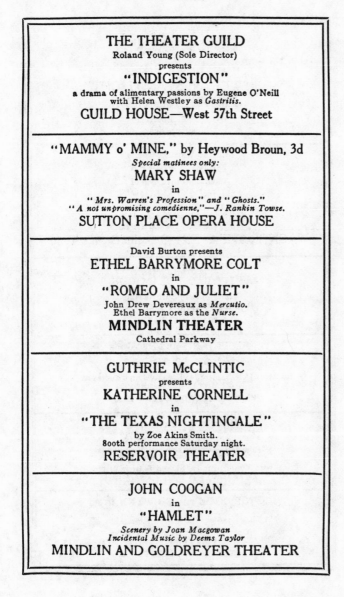

THE THEATER GUILD
Roland Young (Sole Director)
presents
"INDIGESTION"
a drama of alimentary passions by Eugene O'Neill
with Helen Westley as *Gastritis.*
GUILD HOUSE—West 57th Street

"MAMMY o' MINE," by Heywood Broun, 3d
*Special matinees only:*
MARY SHAW
in
" *Mrs. Warren's Profession* " and " *Ghosts.* "
" *A not unpromising comedienne,* "—*J. Rankin Towse.*
SUTTON PLACE OPERA HOUSE

David Burton presents
ETHEL BARRYMORE COLT
in
"ROMEO AND JULIET"
John Drew Devereaux as *Mercutio.*
Ethel Barrymore as the *Nurse.*
MINDLIN THEATER
Cathedral Parkway

GUTHRIE McCLINTIC
presents
KATHERINE CORNELL
in
"THE TEXAS NIGHTINGALE"
by Zoe Akins Smith.
800th performance Saturday night.
RESERVOIR THEATER

JOHN COOGAN
in
"HAMLET"
*Scenery by Joan Macgowan*
*Incidental Music by Deems Taylor*
MINDLIN AND GOLDREYER THEATER

Florenz Ziegfeld
announces the
Return to the Spoken Drama
of

## BILLIE BURKE

### in "SWEETNESS AND LIGHT"

## EMPIRE THEATER

WORLD PREMIÈRE
Christmas Night.

---

Charles Wagner presents

## HELEN HAYES

in an all-star revival of

## "BECKY SHARP"

with Donald Gallaher as *Rawdon*
and Sidney Blackmer as *Steyne*.
*Offstage noises by John McCormack.*

## WAGNER THEATER—Opposite Grant's Tomb

---

THE BOWERY BURLESQUERS

### *in* "MY BAD DREAM GIRL"

Hear Miriam Battista sing

### "When Grandma Was a Boy"

### BELASCO THEATER

---

### ELSIE JANIS and Her Gang

### *in* "ON TO TOKIO"

Mrs. JANIS, mère, will positively *not* appear at
every performance

### VAN CORTLANDT OPERA HOUSE

---

## Charles Frohman, Inc.

(MICHAEL GOLDREYER, Director)
*offers* LESLIE HOWARD *in*
John Drinkwater's new historical drama

## "CALVIN COOLIDGE"

with Wm. A. Brady, 3d, and Patricia Ziegfeld

**EQUITY THEATER**                    Wednesday night

---

### JOE COOK and ED WYNN *in*

### "THE WOWS of 1943"

Opening postponed until Saturday
(*Last Winter's Tickets as good as ever*)

### JEROME PARK THEATER

JOAN STRANGE *in*

"PETER PAN"

**BARRYMORE THEATER**     Opposite Grant's Tomb

---

POCKET THEATER
(127 ½ East 96th Street——Three flights up)
Special Matinees of
**"DA"**
**By ST. JOHN ERVINE**
with (and in spite of) Augustin Duncan
**Both Seats on Sale at the Box Office**

---

MORRIS GEST
bursts with pride in announcing
**THE SIAMESE ART THEATER**
(by arrangement with the Prince of Siam)
*Engagement positively limited to one performance*
**Seats eight weeks in advance**
To be followed next Spring
by
**THE SENEGALESE NATIONAL REPERTORY**
at
**TEMPLE GEST**
*Engagement limited to 4 weeks, God forbid.*

# THE ESSENCE OF ACTING

THE silliest phrase in the jargon of the theater is the expression "an emotional actress," as if there were any other kind. Just how witless it is, you may never realize fully until you inspect its chill co-relative "an unemotional actress," which is a mad contradiction in terms.

The conveyance of emotion is the very essence of acting. Instinctively, every theatergoer knows this. Even the critics know it. But when, in the Spring of the year, they sit down to ponder majestically on their funny little lists of the season's best performances, this knowledge mysteriously deserts them. They are a little bewildered by the vivid and arresting personalities of the year's outstanding players. They feel vaguely that such personalities are never sufficiently submerged in the play's illusion. They drag out the hoary phrase about the actors who "always play themselves," a phrase which has been brandished over them all from Garrick to Ben Ami, a phrase which—and this is worth noting—has been brandished most severely over the best of each generation.

I suspect that the wiseacres at a certain Globe Theater, which was struggling along pretty well before ever Charles Dillingham came on earth, used to take Shakespeare aside and protest to him that this fellow Burbage was much overrated and that he was playing *Othello* just the way he played *Hamlet*. I suspect, furthermore, that Shakespeare smiled and went off by himself to work on that scene of final misery wherewith he was planning to have Burbage voice the downward slope of "King Lear." Just as they fretted because Irving was always Irving and Mansfield always Mansfield, so they fret now because Duse is always Duse, and Mrs. Fiske always Mrs. Fiske. It is quite true, of course. Just as a Debussy composition is unmistakably his or a story by Conrad ever and always a story by Conrad.

But, they ask, isn't it the actor's chief business to vanish utterly behind the character he is playing? To which the answer, unexpected, apparently, is a decided negative. If that were true, if disguise and impersonation were what mattered *most*, then a bushy set of whiskers would be the most important factor in an actor's art. If that were true, then Ruth Draper, who can successively take on the look and manner of an eager young Scotch girl, a rancid old New England crone and a raucous, little Grand Street *Cinderella* all in a quarter hour and all without mask or paint or powder, would have to be recognized as a greater actress than Duse ever was.   No, the actor's chief business is concerned with emotion.   It is to transmit certain states and qualities of the heart and mind.   He deals with such things as fear and anger and courage and heartache.   If he can express them convincingly, nothing else matters much.   If he can't, nothing else helps.

All of which, as a matter of fact, is a part of every playgoer's instinctive and unexplored understanding of the theater.   The youngest usher would have no real uncertainty in the matter if, for instance, he were called on to decide which of three candidates should be chosen for a part.   Let us suppose that the part is that of a young French governess caught in a dangerous trap and panic-stricken.   One of the aspirants might have the youth, another the true French accent.   But the part would go to the actress who had the panic.   Of course it would.

It is not easy to determine just why the critics are forever trying to hide from the fact that acting is essentially an expression of emotion.   Perhaps it has been brought about through the tendency to degrade the term "emotional acting" by reserving it for emotional outbursts, by the foolish notion that the most emotional scene is the one in which emotion is most loudly given way to and that the most emotional actress is the one who sheds the most pints of tears in a season and uses up the largest number of handkerchiefs.   As a matter of fact, the most moving and the most communicable grief is dumb grief; the most devasting tears, in the theater as in life, are the tears unshed.  A freshet on the stage usually induces a severe drought in the audience.

Perhaps, too, they are fiercely though unconsciously resisting all the vainglorious anecdotes which the green room autobiographies yield about the players who could wring sobs from a basilisk by reciting the alphabet in a sufficiently touching manner.  I have always been a little skeptical about such tales—such tales, for instance, as that one of Margaret Anglin weeping compassionately over the fate of a poor, helpless little chocolate eclair which she was about to devour.  Or that older one of Modjeska delivering the Polish multiplication table in a heartrending manner to a deeply aroused American audience.  These tales are usually trotted out by actors to prove how little the playwrights matter, how independent of the dramatist the genuine player is.  They are likely to prove just the opposite.

In his bland and wise little wafer-thin volume "On Acting," Brander Matthews tells this one from Ernesto Rossi, the famous Italian tragedian.  Rossi, it seems, was having supper one evening at Padua with half a dozen fellow-actors, and they fell into a discussion of their own art and its possibilities.

"One of them," says Professor Matthews, "picked up

the bill of fare and declared his intention of reading
this barren list so pathetically as to bring tears to their
eyes.   The other actors refused to believe that this was
possible: they were not credulous spectators: they were
hardened to every trick of the trade; and they smiled
at his proposal.   The first words he read simply, rising
soon to a large dignity of utterance that veiled the
commonplace syllables.   Then his rich, full voice began
to tremble as if with fear, and to quiver at length as
though the soul of the speaker was pierced with poign-
ant agony.   Despite the repugnant words, which ceased
to be perceived clearly, the sweeping emotion with
which his tones were charged proved to be irresistibly
contagious; and long before he had read to the end of the
bill of fare his comrades found themselves looking at
each other with tears rolling down their cheeks."

Now, I am a fairly susceptible playgoer, willing
enough to be carried along by the current of a play and
by the tide of a performance, but I doubt if that exploit
in Padua would have aroused in me more than mild
curiosity.   Indeed, although Professor Matthews does
not make the suggestion, I suspect that on that occasion
Signor Rossi and his friends were all soused to the gills.
In the theaters along Broadway, piece after piece
reminds us all that this business of acting in a vacuum
is singularly uninfectious and that the most expressive
and most imaginative of players cannot make good out

of their own resources a basic lack of validity in the scene committed to them.

This dependence of the actor's art was, as I recall it now, first forcibly driven in on me by a Hall Caine melodrama called "Margaret Schiller," in which the lovely and talented Miss Ferguson sobbed and raved and died and so forth in a most skillful manner, which, however, left us all quite glacial in our detachment. "Margaret Schiller," you see, was one of those preposterous plays of synthetic excitement which manages to last all evening on the pretense that every one in the piece is a defective and that the audience will not be any too bright, either. It was contrived by one of those elaborate plots which would go all to pieces if, by any chance, any of its characters betrayed for one moment a grain of common sense. *Margaret Schiller* was ruthlessly thrust into the most painful and harrowing predicaments, but it was not within Elsie Ferguson's power to make them seem to matter. It was just as though we had seen the fair damsel walk resolutely out on to a railroad track and seat herself deliberately in the path of an oncoming locomotive. Thereafter she might cower and tremble and weep all she wished without arousing any deeper response than a mild wonder as to why the poor moron did not get up and walk away.

# THE DISSENTER

In a disappointing and undependable world, one thing, at least, is immutable. One thing can be counted on. That is the Dissenter. In criticism he springs up as promptly and as inevitably as one end of a see-saw springs up when, with authority and conviction, you plant yourself firmly on the other. Enthusiasm once expressed, for any act or thing or word or person, creates by its own draught, its own minute report. If you go down into the market place and throw up your hat in artless joy over someone's achievement, you will, if you listen attentively, hear a near-by desk snap shut and the clatter of somebody hustling down the stairs blissfully intent on denying that that achievement amounted to much—determined, if need be, to insist that it amounted to nothing at all.

This phenomenon of the human species is especially familiar in the theater. There, in the flux of shifting standards and hazy terms, the professional Dissenter has the time of his young life. Feed him a little pot of after-dinner coffee, and five or six names from the roster of the most belaureled favorites of the hour, and he is

good for the evening.    Then you will hear what twiddle
Barrie writes and how inept a creature is Marie Jeritza
in "Tosca."

If he is given to scribbling, he becomes identified with
some weekly or monthly publication.    None of these
snap judgments for him of course.    Your Dissenter
needs a little leisure, if not for rich meditation, then at
least to find out which way the wind is blowing.    One
difficulty in taking your stand with the minority lies in
the tedious necessity of waiting to learn how the yokelry
of the majority will vote.

It is quite simple.    Let us say that the flourishing
Lisa Ondarcho has come to us from Milan.    Her first
American audience finds her lovely and eloquent and
genuinely moving.    The hurried scribes of the dailies,
thankful for that much manna in a wilderness of first
nights, do a little roaring next day.    The reviewer of
the stanch little magazine, the *Scarlatina*, reads their
efforts and, while the messenger waits, does a bit of
automatic writing for his department in the next issue.
In a few incisive paragraphs he effectually disposes of
the Ondarcho's absurd pretensions.    He points out
that she is vulgar and blatant.    He says, moreover,
that she is a dull girl.    He suggests that had she been a
native-born actress she would have been assigned to
character parts in the stock company of Rahway, New
Jersey.    He opines that if the nincompoops of the
dailies had ever really studied the present-day theater

in Italy—if, for instance, they had seen the 1920 revival of "Il Vero Amico" with Travina and the saucy little Cannuchi—they would have known that there are a dozen unpretentious young mimes playing there now, each one of them immeasurably superior to the Ondarcho. And so on and so on. It is, you see, a formula which any one can work. You do not even have to have been in Italy. A clipping service can lend anyone the aureole of the globe-trotter. Simple and steadfast reliance on this formula has kept more than one scribe in gin and taxis for many a season. And it must be admitted that more than once it has led right smack into the truth.

So since the Dissenter is always with us, it is small wonder, for instance, that one heard from time to time that this Chauve-Souris of the round Balieff was, as their phrase goes, the bunk. That good and modest and artful little show of his gave so much genuine satisfaction that a few condescending speeches and pieces on its pathetic mediocrity were among the things that just had to be.

The arguments employed for the purpose were, however, a little curious. Those which caught these eyes dwelt most fondly on the idea that here was an artful bit of Muscovite vaudeville, a miscellany of numbers very like those given in our musical comedies and variety halls—only in the "Chauve-Souris," they were better done. Ordinary stuff, we take it, only better done. That the "Parade of the Wooden Soldier" was similar to many a musical number staged again and again along Broadway—only better done.

What justified all that hullabaloo about *Trilby's* singing? She sang the most ordinary of old nursery songs. And her only contribution was that she sang them better than they had ever been sung before. It made one regret a light headed enthusiasm for the Ballet Russe when one recalled that, after all, the dancing which Nijinski and Lopokova did for that troupe was just like the dancing of many less overrated hoofers in our own vaudeville houses. Only better done. As for the phrases which Verlaine left behind him, what are they? No more than Mr. Guest can turn out by the gross every morning before breakfast. Only better done.

That is the phrase over whose astounding implications we keep stumbling. It is really slipped in so casually, as though it really modified the context insignificantly, like saying that Henry VIII. was a good husband, only somewhat given to wife murder. Or that one's fiancée is a sweet girl with no bad habits, except of course, mayhem. Only better done, forsooth. As the great magnate so well expresses it in one of Mr. Squire's little dramas—"Pah!"

# A FEW ANNOYING DRAMAS

So many of the plays which a New York reviewer must see each season in his sentry duty along Broadway might easily be dismissed with a word were it not for the repertorial instinct and habit which is in all of us. Deems Taylor (who, though belabored somewhat elsewhere in these pages, did, after all, suggest the title for this volume) is always threatening to replace his usual review of the music of the day with some such paragraph as this one:

"Alfredo Cellani's 'Loreley' was produced last evening at the Metropolitan. What of it?"

But he never does. Though Ernest Lawford does delight to tell how an English critic once commented on one of his own youthful appearances in an obscure rôle in London. "Mr. Lawford," the notice ran, "was cast as *Lord Littledale*. Why?"

From the reviewer's standpoint, the difficult task is not the fine play or the terrible play. It is the piece that is neither one nor the other. I find among my notes some records of these more annoying dramas.

Here, lest you think a critic's life is a bed of roses, are several:

## I.—"LA TENDRESSE"

We often wonder how familiar a reaction among theatergoers is our own immediate mutiny at an implausible incident in a play. The rebellion becomes violent when such a special strain on the credulity occurs in the very climax of the piece and is caused by a device lugged in to complete the playwright's fond plan for a theatrically effective scene, calculated to make Sardou writhe with envy in his grave. Past such arbitrary devices, the playwrihgt seems to scuttle hurriedly, murmuring to himself, like the deluded players in "The Torch Bearers":

"I don't believe the audience noticed it."

This particular part of the audience notices it no more than he would a grain of dust in his eye. Such a grain of dust seriously affected our vision at "La Tendresse," a searching and genuinely human play by that most leisurely and verbose of modern French dramatists—the late Henry Bataille. It is one of those characteristically Parisian plays that depict the woe of a gray, infirm and sentimental fellow when (to his quite inexplicable surprise) he finds that his young mistress has been dallying à côté with a hot-blooded youngster selected from among her own contemporaries. To such a tale of woe our own instinctive response is always "What of it?" But it is a subject on which your French playwright in his declining years invariably works up a

considerable inner agitation, and, as you listen to his
scenes unfold, you can almost hear the steady drip-drip-
drip of his sympathetic tears.

In "La Tendresse," the old chap (acted by Henry
Miller) is *Paul Barnac*, the foremost playwright of his
day.  And the lady who thus tears his heart .by her
infidelity is a lovely, bouncing, young actress (capitally
played by Ruth Chatterton) who skips rope and sits
archly on the floor and is generally, one would think,
rather a nuisance around the house.  To *Barnac* in his
happiness come some friends, who tell him (the dear,
helpful chaps) that the lady is cheating.  Having gone
thus far, one of them develops a sudden belated scruple
and won't name the rival or rivals.  Would he at least
give the initial?  No.  Then would he *write* the initial
on a slip of paper?  Well, for reasons not quite clear,
that seems less tale-bearing and he agrees.  But just to
make it harder, he puts down the wrong initial—the
letter G.

So *Barnac*, after gloomily studying his address-book,
selects two potentially guilty G's, makes appointments
for them at his house next day, bribes his stenographer
to hide behind the curtain and then pretends to leave
town.  The next act deals with the suspensive but
inconclusive visits of these two reluctant innocents.
Then, by accident and for the first time in his life, the
real offender chances to come a-calling, and, with the
stenographer presumably having the time of her life

behind the curtain, there ensues an extremely incriminating five-minute dialogue.

This is not yet over when *Barnac* telephones to announce his return and a few moments later in he comes and stages a torture scene. In his hand are four or five pages of manuscript which he pretends to have dashed off for his next play on the train that afternoon. Would she mind testing them by reading them aloud— or at least reading the woman's speeches aloud the while he cues her from memory? Puzzled at his manner, she agrees and then you see her cringe and cower as she falters out the first lines. They are the guilty lines she had spoken a little while before in that very room.

Whereupon the play flares up in a briny scene of recrimination and despair that keeps on and on and on, with the abject woman starting for the door and coming back, starting for the door and coming back, like Gilbert's insufficiently intrepid police sergeant, till you want to cry out in the words of Major General Stanley:

"But you *don't* go."

And all through this scene at its first New York performance we kept wondering how in the name of Isaac Pitman he had managed in so brief a time to lay hands on the legibly transcribed script of that evil dialogue, read it, go out, telephone to her to scare the lover away and then come back with his little plot all laid. To be sure, *Barnac* muttered something about there having been two stenographers—the need of such speed and the recklessness of engaging an outsider are unexplained—but even this seemed inadequate. This grain of dust maddened us so that M. Bataille's big scene became a three-cornered one that ran something— a little something—like this.

He—How could you have deceived me so?

She—Darling, I loved you all the time.

*We (to ourselves)—Those stenographers must have been marvelous.*

He—Why didn't you tell me?

She—Darling, I was too base, too cowardly.

*We—One of them might have taken it down directly on a typewriter, but then we would have heard the machine.*

He—I trusted you so completely.

She—I was unworthy.

*We—But perhaps it was a noiseless typewriter.*

He—I wish you were dead at my feet.

She—I wish I were.

*We—No, come to think of it, he says the writing is in long hand.*

He—Go. I never want to see you again.

She—It's terribly hard for me to explain.

*We—We should think it would be. Why they must have worked it in relays, but when we used to cover mid-night speeches for the first edition, there were never any stenographers around who could tear it off like that.*

He (*choking her and throwing her on the chaise-lounge*)
—WANTON!

*We—Fast workers!    Fast workers!*

## II.—"MANHATTAN"

From time to time it is acrimoniously argued that
the reviewers ought not measure the passing plays by
their own perverse and epicurean taste nor commit
themselves by applying any adjectives whatever—such
as hilarious, febrile, dainty, narcotic, repulsive or the
like—to the new piece of the night before.   As a matter
of fact, while much would be lost, something might be
gained by barring adjectival indulgence from journal-
istic criticism, like firmly telling the cook that there
must be no more thickening in the soup.   One of the
scribes, for instance, rather induced the impression that
every new play was worth seeing the first six months
after his first encounter with the word "intriguing" and
the remote Louis Sherwin (before he shut his eyes, held
his nose and jumped into the movies) was so abjectly
devoted to the word "jejune" that he would lick it and
paste it on every new play whether it was in the least
jejune or not.

However, as we understand the contention, the
desideratum is a severe, impersonal description of the
play.   Now it is quite impossible to accomplish that in
terms of the first-night reception.   If a first-nighter

is pleased and entertained, he beats his palms together and laughs till he almost falls into the aisle. But watch him when he is bored. Then he beats his palms together and laughs till he almost falls into the aisle. So one is driven relentlessly back to bare description of the play's contents, its fabric, its design—in short, its plot.

Let us then consider the plot of the piece called "Manhattan," which launched one season at the Playhouse. The curtain rises on the library of the Van Norman home in Park Avenue. (It has been several years now since any dramatist has sheltered his more elegant characters on Riverside Drive or on Fifth or Madison Avenue. Only Clare Kummer—ever a bit wild and puckish in her fancy—has had the pioneer spirit to break from this tradition. Once, only once— it was in "The Robbery"—she went so far as to set the scene *in a cross street*. However, in most plays all the best people live on Park Avenue.)

Well, the aforesaid rising curtain reveals *Duncan Van Norman* busy writing an essay for *The Atlantic Monthly*. He is doing this in a snuggery so conveniently close to the front door that the butler has scarce disappeared in response to the door-bell when the room is a-swarm with laughing society folk, all eager to drag him off to some gayety. The *Van Normans*, as far as the play reveals, are a family of three—widowed mother, son and daughter. They have two bookcases and a butler. When *Miss Van Norman* has a burst of confidence, she does not skip up the plebeian stairs to her mother's boudoir and begin: "Mom, *what* do you think has happened?" Not she. Instead she rings for the butler and says: "*Paget*, tell my mother I wish to see her in the library and talk to her about something I want the audience to overhear." No, come to think of it, the last part of that sentence isn't actually spoken.

Well, *Duncan* isn't in the best of health. This is evidenced by his announcing that he does not care for any dinner beyond a biscuit and a glass of port—a dietetic arrangement which the authors in some way subtly associate with his writings for *The Atlantic*. However, both manifestations worry his gaudy old mother, who tries to persuade him that it is high time for him to go forth and cut up a bit. The same advice is then echoed by the family lawyer, who sends him a pretty little typist with the suggestion that he might seduce her, and, presumably, thereby become a contributor to *The Saturday Evening Post*. The typist arrives. She proves to be young, personable, poor. She is *Peg-o-My-Heart* all over again and again and again. She lacks the brogue and the red hair and Michael, to be sure, but she says "Gee" quite often; she is fond of poetry and she is so hard up that she agrees to copy "The Fourth Dimension in Ethics" for *The Atlantic*.

She copies it in a wretched little garret room south of

Greenwich Village, which she shares with an Irish miss.
This colleen is the good-natured kind who gives all her
dinner to the poor starving girl next door. One gathers
from the chit-chat of these three that a poor working-
girl in New York has only to say the word—the word
is "Yes"—to have sables and limousines galore. Indeed, one of their little circle appears to have said
"Yes" recently, and they are all speculating on her
happiness and wondering whether it was worth the
price. There is some difference of opinion. Enter
*Duncan Van Norman*. His arrival at this lowly spot
might take the unsophisticated unawares, but the canny
first-nighter knows full well that no manager, who has
worked himself up to the point of paying Norman
Trevor's salary, would ever allow an act to slip by
without using him. Metaphorically speaking, *Duncan*
has come in with a sable coat in one hand and a limou-
sine in the other. He also mentions art, music, travel.
He is spurned by the typist, who, however, does get
five hundred dollars out of him for the poor starving
girl next door and does consent to become his secretary.

The next act sees her thus installed in Park Avenue,
where she takes hints from *Paget* and reads assiduously
in *The Book of Etiquette*, all in an effort to "become a
lady." Indeed, how she ever escaped from a novel by
Frances Hodgson Burnett is one of the mysteries of
modern letters. Well, naturally, you can imagine the
talk caused in what the *Van Normans* call either "our

world" or "the circle in which we move," when it is
bruited up and down Park Avenue that *Duncan Van
Norman* has a female secretary who comes right to his
library every day and does his typing.   There is so
much scandal that *Duncan* offers marriage on the spot,
which, despite his mother's efforts to buy the girl off,
might settle matters and obviate the necessity of a last
act, when in rushes that old family lawyer again, this
time not to suggest that *Duncan* seduce some one else,
but with the news that the little typist has just that
moment inherited $450,000 of South African real estate.
Of course, *Duncan* is horribly embarrassed by that,
but she lands him at last by the expedient of locking
herself in a room with him and throwing the key out
the window.

And there you are.   Though why "Manhattan?"
To be sure, the scenes are *not* in Tallahassee, but
then on that principle "Hamlet" might as well be
called "Denmark" and "The First Year" might as
well have been renamed "Redding, Illinois, and Joplin,
Missouri."   Why "Manhattan," do you suppose?
Let's see.   It's the name of an island and of a borough
and of a transfer and of a cocktail and—oh, yes—of a
storehouse.

### III.—"MORPHIA"

Although it is an unbelievably gauche and artless
play, the piece called "Morphia," which was offered

tentatively one afternoon at the Eltinge Theater, does have in it one of those writhing and twisting rôles of hysteria which all actors love to play. The temptations of that rôle proved much too strong for the facile Lowell Sherman.

One can imagine his instant recognition of the play as a preposterously false and garish bit of theatrical trash. One can picture him hurling it from him several times and finally locking it in his bookcase, where the sight of it would not madden him. One can guess how he paced the floor, his slender, eloquent hands clenched above his head, sweat beading the interesting pallor of his brow. "No," he must have muttered between clamped teeth, "I will not. I will not. I will not."

But there it lay—that tempting, showy rôle, with its chance to out-twitch Master Barrymore, with its tumultuous love scenes and with its triumphant third act proof that love is stronger than morphine. It was too much. Too much for almost any actor. Too much, certainly, for Lowell Sherman. Uttering a low, heart-rending cry, he snatched the play to his bosom, rushed to the Eltinge Theater and acted it all over the stage.

This Mr. Sherman is an actor of such natural endowment and such exceptional facility that the intelligent playgoers are forever haunted by the suspicion that they could make use of him in the kind of plays they like to

see. As far as we could recall, most of his associations
had been with the rubbishy plays which do not matter
and which keep all the actors involved in them from
mattering in the least. Thus Mr. Sherman did not
matter. In that respect he is like most of our players.
But he differs from most in his constant provocation of
the notion that he might matter.

"Possibly," we all said, "if he were ever seen in a fine
rôle in a fine play his now invisible inadequacies would
become suddenly and painfully apparent. That sometimes happens and the effect is the effect that morning
sunlight has on a cracked and shoddy window blind.
But perhaps, on the other hand, he would emerge as
one of the significant and respected players of our
theater. We shall see. Rumors associate his name
with a revival of 'Richard the Third' and with the rôle
of *Casanova*, which is to be acted by some one at the
Empire next season."

Well, we saw. As *Casanova*, Mr. Sherman was,
frankly, pretty bad—incorrigibly actory throughout
and so alien to the brocades and periwigs of the Eighteenth Century that, as some one said, he seemed to be
always looking for a telephone.

"Morphia" appears to be a heated work from the
German, done over for us by a Scotchman. It rehearses
the rescue of a morphine addict by a boyhood
sweetheart who, many years after their idyll, comes to
him disguised as a nurse and, in the climax of the piece

(the scene where Mr. Sherman's cue is to wallow on the floor and paw her in his distraction), offers to slake his appetites with something else than morphine if he will give his word of honor never to touch the drug again. "Morphia" may be described as the kind of play which proceeds upon the theory that an addict is safe once he has given his word of honor.

Furthermore, it is the kind of play in which he says that the sunset makes London look like a fairy city and her like a fairy princess. And, as if to match such dialogue and all the transparent folderol by which the plot is set wheezing to work, the stage-craft that afternoon was equally preposterous—from the loving care with which the little homebody put flowers in all the vases (without the idea ever popping into her pretty head that one also needed water on such occasions) to the extraordinarily permanent sunset which suggested that the stage manager was none other than Joshua. Such didoes, when accompanied by the arrestingly theatricalized acting of all the supporting players, made the whole enterprise seem stagey. Indeed, when Mr. Sherman gazed out into the aforesaid setting and asked, "What is that I see out there?" one half expected Olive Tell to murmur, "That, dear heart, is old Al Woods."

### IV.—"SANDRO BOTTICELLI"

The biographical drama called "Sandro Botticelli," which was earnestly projected one evening from the tiny stage of the Provincetown Theater, was a pretentious piece, skimpily and artlessly put together, which, despite an ambitious and sometimes excellent performance, teetered unconsciously on the verge of the ridiculous. It was the first play by Mercedes De Acosta and it was impossible to sit through it, embedded in the elegant but unenthusiastic audience that attended the dress rehearsal, without wondering if it ever would have reached the light even of Macdougal Street had it been the maiden work of Mamie Snooks of Nowhere in Particular.

What Miss De Acosta did was to take a Botticelli legend from a short story by Maurice Hewlett and make it into an awkward little play in five scenes, wherein some pretty high stepping language was made to mingle with the conventional Won't-you-sit-downs of modern comedy and in which an essentially farcical situation was made the crux of a romantically melancholy drama. What she did not do, apparently, was to read the tonic derision of just such stuff in Max Beerbohm's "Seven Men."

The piece was helped along by Basil Sidney's admirable playing as *Botticelli* and now helped, now hindered by the creditable but severely handicapped performance of Eva Le Gallienne as *Simonetta*. Miss Le Gallienne played with forthright honesty and conviction and was excellent in the death scene, but, cast as the lustrous and inciting beauty of Florence, she looked so incorrigibly childlike that in that death scene she was less *Botticelli's* lady than *Hannele.*

The play's first audience on Sunday evening was superbly self-controlled, despite the play's many temptations to unmannerly laughter. Laughter lurks in the very central episode where *Simonetta* goes nude to *Botticelli's* studio (a scene neatly managed by veiling her with the actress's hair and an intervening armchair). She, who is given to talking a good deal about the beauty of her body, goes to him on the pretense that she wants that beauty handed down through the ages on an immortal canvas and she is furiously indignant when she finds out that painting her was, as a matter of fact, all that the handsome young artist was minded to do to her.

This frustration of hers drives her out into the storm of rain-swept Florence and she never recovers from the resulting delirium. While the play is pervaded with the illusion that she dies of thwarted love and wounded self-esteem, it is rather intimated that, according to the concensus of medical opinion in Florence, a not inexplicable cold had had something to do with it. Now here, we take it, is an inherently comic illustration of the ancient dilemma between art and love, but the author of "Sandro Botticelli" was deadly serious as she wrote.

Laughter lurks, too, in the preposterous sense of huddle given by the Provincetown stage to the garden of Lorenzo the Magnificent, which must have been imagined by the playwright as a stately and spacious plaisaunce, but which, under the conditions, provoked the old inquiry as to how many angels could sit on the point of a pin, and recalled less a plaisaunce than the washroom of a sleeper in the last half hour before the Grand Central.

It was this scene which incited so persistently the memory of the burlesque historical drama called "Savonarola," which Max Beerbohm composed for "Seven Men." In its great third act, at the peak of the confrontation of *Savonarola* with *Lucrezia Borgia*, the script reads thus·

" (*Savonarola* throws ring in *Lucrezia's* face. Enter *Pope Julius II.* with Papal army.)

"*Pope*—Arrest that man and woman.

" (Reënter Guelfs and Ghibellines fighting. *Savonarola* and *Lucrezia* are arrested by Papal officers. Enter *Michael Angelo*. *Andrea del Sarto* appears for a moment at a window. *Pippa* passes. Brothers of the Miserecordia go by, singing a requiem for *Francesca da Rimini*. Enter *Boccaccio*, *Benvenuto Cellini* and many others, making remarks highly characteristic of themselves, but scarcely audible throughout the terrific thunder which now bursts over Florence and is at its loudest as the curtain falls.)"

It was of "Savonarola Brown" that we all must

have thought as the curtain rose and *Lorenzo dei Medici*, *Leonardo da Vinci*, *Fra Filippo Lippi*, *Simonetta* and *Botticelli* were identified as a few of those busy squeezing themselves on to the Provincetown stage. This Mr. Beerbohm is a disturbing fellow and, as just one of his pieces of mischief, he has made it definitely difficult to attend Miss De Acosta's honest effort with a perfectly straight face.

# THE INCAUTIOUS DRAMA

IF the crowds did not precisely storm the doors of the theaters where two such hopeful dramas as "Scaramouche" and "The Cup" were playing it was due, among other causes, to the fact that neither play made much use of the power of suggestion. Neither playwright left anything to the imagination of his audience. And yet, for all Augustus Thomas's recent observations about the high percentage of morons among his fellow citizens, there are many times when the stimulated mind of the simplest playgoer so leaps ahead of the action on the stage that the most glowing actor, panting like the *Red Queen* in the garden, has a desperate time in his pathetic efforts merely to keep up with it.

For the more obvious of such occasions there are all manner of danger signals set up by bitter past experience. When a director has such a play as "Trilby" to stage, for instance, one signal flutters scarlet for all to see. That is the play about the simple, good hearted young grisette whom a mesmeric musician converts into such a singer as none had ever heard, a singer at whose concerts the whole world weeps from sheer delight,

213

and compared with whose golden notes the notes of Patti and Jenny Lind seem ordinary. The most literal and unimaginative director would know that, with a single exception, the actress engaged for that part might do anything she liked. She might, if so minded, dance a highland fling, talk with a German accent or fall on her face from time to time. But she must not sing. The voice of voices must be dreamed and not heard. Even if a Midas management could engage the greatest singer from the Metropolitan to warble in the wings it would seem a poor thing compared with the imagined voice that we out front were really listening to. And yet when "Trilby" was last given in our town a strapping young English actress named Phyllis Neilson Terry had the hardihood to step before the curtain and pipe sweetly —to the utter undoing of the play.

Once upon a time there was staged in our town a modest comedy about a Russian ballerina, who, in a careless moment, had married a young gentleman from the Berkshires. A not untalented and not uncomely actress played the part, the art of the ballerina was taken for granted, and all was well on the first night until the climax of the play, when we, in the audience, noted with a kind of frozen horror that she was getting up on her toes. What followed in the next moment was one of the most acutely embarrassing experiences we had ever suffered in the theater.

Yet, lo, untaught by such familiar mishaps, behold

Master Sabatini writing a play for the young and
aspiring and talented Sidney Blackmer.  Blackmer,
though his caressing speech does suggest that Brittany
is rather nearer No'th Ca'lina than we had suspected,
was not a bad choice for Sabatini's skirmisher.  But
the author set him at least one impossible task.  In the
second act of that romance of the French Revolution
*Scaramouche* is hiding in a Breton barn, a fugitive from
justice, because by a flaming and inflammable speech
at Rennes the week before he had set the torch to the
tinder of the Breton discontent and roused the mob to
murder.  One is quite willing to believe that all this
happened until, in a dizzy moment of creative vanity,
Sabatini actually ventures to have the second act turn
on a repetition of that speech within full sight and hearing of the audience.  The result is disastrous.  True
the speech happens to have been translated into hopelessly ineloquent English.  True Mr. Blackmer does
not as yet combine all the arts and wiles of Lucien
Guitry, John Barrymore and Ivan Moskvin.  True, too,
that his fellow players do not always coöperate to the
extent of seeming spellbound.  Indeed, on one occasion,
we saw one of them—was it H. Cooper-Cliffe?—
strangely interested in the property food that was
before him.  And the gaze of the insouciant Kerrigan
was not fixed on *Scaramouche*.  Not at all.  It was
fixed inquisitively on the tenth row aisle.  But what of
it?  Had Wendell Phillips written the speech and

Edwin Booth risen from his grave to speak it, probably
when the intermission came we should all have gone out
into the lobby wondering what the people in Rennes
had been so excited about. No defect in the writing,
acting and staging of that speech is comparable with
the crushing defect of its having been staged at all.

A similar hardihood considerably weakened the
potentially stirring miracle play called "The Cup."
William Hurlbut started out with a most drama laden
idea—that notion that the Holy Grail, lost through the
weary centuries, should come to light in such a gathering place of publicans and sinners as a thief's flat off our
own Bowery. And one seldom finds in the theater
a more tingling moment than that one when the cheerful burglar comes home and by sundry devices of the
playwright you know, though he does not, what price-
less treasure is in the mysterious black box tucked
under his unconscious arm. His girl, a shabby little
East Side Magdalen, divines it, and the second act is
the act of her martyrdom to save it. After she has
hidden it and locked her lips he beats her to insensibility,
and she is lying bruised and bleeding on the floor when
he leaves her for dead. Then, whimpering and frightened, she lifts her head at last. Her eyes widen. Still
kneeling, she stares and stares at the wall in front of her.
The eyes tell of wonder, fear, exaltation. You know
what she sees. But the author is afraid you do not.
So, just before the curtain falls, the wall grows trans-

parent and through it every one, including the head usher, is permitted to behold a fearfully stagey embodiment of the Christ, done in the true tradition of the little chromos which, distributed in thousands upon thousands of Sunday schools throughout this land, must have done so much to weaken the force of Christianity in America.

Untaught by the feebleness of this device, Brother Hurlbut plunged on to a repetition of it. He must have noted how awesome, how dramatic, how real the very presence of the Grail on the stage seemed—*so long as it was not actually visible*. The thief tore at the box lid, plunged his hands down into the velvet wrappings within and saw—what? The answer was written in each face that looked. So long as the cup remained in that box its spell on the audience was extraordinary. But just at the end of the play the priest lifted it out. There it was, heavy, intricate, reeking of Fifth Avenue. And the spell went out the window.

We sometimes are minded to take Mr. Hurlbut, Mr. Sabatini and a few others who might be named on a round of the theaters to show them how much can be said in a few words, how stirring a mere suggestion can be. We should take them to "Queen Victoria," a play that is remarkable for the things the authors were strong enough to leave out of it. We should take them to "The Swan," a romance of such reticent craftsmanship that one little kiss and one draining of a cup of wine are made to seem such thunderclaps as Mr. Hurlbut, with all his bludgeonings, and Mr. Sabatini, with all his shouts, were unable to achieve.

Above all, we should insist on their reading the canny Drinkwater's new play—not the stately "Robert E. Lee," but "Oliver Cromwell." It should be read if only for one scene, the execution of Charles I., for which so many of our showmen would clear an enormous stage, rear a great scaffold, crowd the play with two hundred richly costumed supers and all but pass the ax around the audience to let each playgoer feel its edge. Drinkwater sets his scene in the living room of *Cromwell's* house. You can tell from the murmured speech of his family that the hour is come. Even *Cromwell's* old mother hobbles toward the window and peers out onto the snowclad roofs of old London. *Cromwell*, you gather, is out in the thick of things, but the only reference to him is his mother's reassurance that his overcoat has been sent on after him. Then suddenly the faint hum of voices in some distant square rises in a sharp crescendo. At that telltale sound *Mrs. Cromwell* goes back to the fireplace, muttering to herself: "Poor, silly king." There is a painful pause, and *Cromwell*, unnoticed, comes into the room. The group at the window does not turn. He walks silently to his mother's armchair and, leaning on its back, stands looking, as she is looking, into the embers on the hearth. The curtain falls.

It is at plays like "The Cup" that we meditate afresh on abandoning newspaper work and going in for stage direction. An intelligent and sovereign director could have made that piece of Mr. Hurlbut's into another "Rain." One would only have to lock the manager out of the theater and blindfold the author and throw him into the cellar. After that a little judicious cutting would do the trick.

It is true that in these hypothetical directions of ours we are prone to forget that the actors might resist. They are incalculable factors, of course. One play, which a little cutting might have saved, was not saved because the impossible speeches assigned to the leading woman could not be touched. You see, the author had complicated rehearsals by falling in love with her. Then there are certain stars who will permit all speeches to be cut except their own, which they feel simply cannot be too long to satisfy their public. It has been said of one of them, who is of English birth, that any playwright could send a rôle to him with the comfortable feeling that none of it would be left out on the opening night—except the h's.

# THE HELPFUL DRAMA

SOMETIMES a play on which New York has smiled sets forth confidently on a coast to coast tour and gets no further than Newark. The time has come to mention the fact that "The Fool," over which a considerable part of New York both smiled and wept, found even greater favor in the provinces. Philadelphia, Chicago and points west have taken it to their hearts, and three other companies are playing it to vast profits. Channing Pollock wrote a simple, hard-hitting play about a man who, in a discouraging world, tried to live like Christ. As we recall, Mr. Pollock's hero gave all his money to the poor. And the author is now in the perhaps embarrassing position of having made a great fortune already from this piece—a fortune which was clearly destined to pass before its second June the sum of $500,000.

Memories of "The Fool" have been stirred by the extraordinary booklet which recounts its history—the tale of its takings and its effects on people. An amazingly variegated list of those who have applauded it is printed, page after page, each page with a little slogan at the top all its own. Thus, under the caption "The Play That Succeeded in Spite of the Devil," one notes that it reached the hearts of De Wolf Hopper, Mrs. A. H. Woods, Dr. Nicholas Murray Butler and Ferdinand Pinney Earle. One (this one) notes with considerable gratification that his own, as well as Alan Dale's encomiums, are quoted under the heading, "And the Wisest Men Enjoy It." Then the praise of such playgoers as Samuel Hopkins Adams, Oliver Herford, Montague Glass, Augustus Thomas, John S. Sumner and Mrs. J. Christopher Marks of the Theater Assembly are all acknowledged under the heading "A Child Can Understand It."

But more interesting still are the sample chronicles of the good "The Fool" has done. Here are a few:

No. 1—A man whose wife was divorcing him sent a copy of "The Fool" to her in Reno. The play brought about a reunion.

No. 2—A college boy, defiant and about to be expelled, saw "The Fool." "I've got a new idea of life," he wrote—and graduated with honors.

No. 3—A Chicago merchant telegraphed a clergyman in his home town, Hinsdale, Ill., to send four boys through college at his expense and give the credit to "The Fool."

No. 4—A woman who had been living illicitly four years with a man who was not her husband saw "The Fool" and refused to return to him.

No. 7—Convict C 1732 in Eastern Penitentiary asked for the play to help remold his character before leaving prison.

We have transcribed these here, not in any doubt of their authenticity, nor in order to point out maliciously, in response to Chronicle No. 1, that the first actor to play the Messianic rôle has since been hauled into the divorce courts, nor in any doubt that "The Fool" has worked a thousand such miracles, but to provoke in any passing reader's mind the speculation as to what plays, after all, do good.   There seem to be many notions on the subject.   For instance, on an incoming postcard which contains a singularly owlish picture of Master Blackmer in his latest rôle, Dr. Frank Crane is quoted as saying:

"Such a play as 'Scaramouche' makes us realize how beautiful a thing is the human heart, and how persistently divine."

Our own notion is that no speech ever written for the stage in our tongue so rings in the heart and could so bless the world if listened to as the blazing retort which *Hamlet* makes to *Polonius* when that smug old nuisance avows an intention to treat the players according to their deserts.   And, if it be good to add a little to the store of pity and compassionate understanding in the world, there is, we think, no play in our town which is so good as "Rain."

It would not be in character for the Theater Guild to

pretend that "The Failures" did good, unless perhaps its directors think that good is served whenever something is wrought with unflinching honesty and austere beauty.  We did not expect the Guild to put out a pamphlet about "The Failures" to vie with the one which rehearses the tonic values of "The Fool."   And yet, come to think of it, we would not put it above the naughties who direct the Guild to have issued a small one making such claims as these:

No. 1—A necktie salesman, who had lived reputably with his wife for nine years, was taken by her to see "The Failures."   She has not seen him since.

No. 2—A burglar, who had just served ten years in Sing Sing, went to see "The Failures" and wrote the warden asking if he could not come back to prison.

No. 3—A Hamilton College sophomore, who saw "The Failures" during the Thanksgiving recess, decided to overstay his leave and see "The Follies," which, though misled by careless reading of the posters, he had meant to see all along.

No. 4—A four-year-old girl, who was taken to "The Failures" by mistake, bit her grandmother between the acts.

# MAETERLINCK

WE came away from "Pelleas and Melisande" with a renewed feeling that, in our own theater, we should be glad to have the rôles of *Paolo* and *Francesca*, however named, played always by Rollo Peters and Jane Cowl. Here was the story of the unhappy lovers told again in a play which for all its success in opera had not been given here since Mrs. Patrick Campbell played it for two performances back in her tanbark era twenty years ago, and which is served this time with all the sorcery of lovely fabrics and color, fine light and the best of acting.

But another feeling was renewed, another conviction deepened—the conviction that this Maurice Maeterlinck is, as the quaint phrase goes, the bunk. Surely this fellow, with his darkling mood and his ornate, sententious simplicity, is little more than one who calculates carefully each flutter in the bosom of the Ladies' Wednesday Afternoon Literary and Chitchat Club in every Gopher Prairie in the world.

In the steady light of so fine and so beautiful a performance as was his portion this time, the somber hangings of the Maeterlinck stage become suddenly recognizable as nothing more nor less than our old friend, the aceldama. And evermore now the sedulous symbolist from hapless Belgium will seem just a little brother to the dank *Bunthorne* who sang:

> Oh, to be wafted away
> From this black aceldama of sorrow,
> Where the earth of a dusty to-day
> Is the dust of an earthy to-morrow.

"A little thing of my own," *Bunthorne* said, as he waved a wistful farewell with the sunflower in his hand. "I call it 'Heart Foam.' I shall *not* publish it."

The precious poet who wrote this tragedy and your usually docile correspondent part company forever at that moment when the mighty *Golaud*, in a very transport of jealous rage, seizes the fair and frightened *Melisande* by the coils of her golden hair, shakes her as one might a teasing kitten, drags her around the castle, meditates on bashing her brains out, decides *not* to, and then hurls her to the flagstones and lets her lie there quivering at his feet. It is only after he has gone that she recovers breath enough to comment on his attitude toward her. Then, with what seems to us a really inadequate faculty of critical expression, she says: "I am unhappy."

And though Jane Cowl can fill the scene with love and foreboding, and though she has brought back some wonder from the moonlit reaches of the *Capulet* garden, and though there are new and lovely cadences that her voice found in Verona, at this point in the woe of *Melisande* one of her most ardent admirers was unable to pay the tribute of anything more or less than a giggle. When *Ophelia*, bidden by the distraught *Hamlet* to get her to a nunnery, tells him she finds his remarks just a wee bit discourteous, when *Desdemona* pries loose the murderous hands from her throat long enough to murmur: "*Othello*, you do flutter me so!"—then, and not before, shall we go hat in hand to another performance of "Pelleas and Melisande."

But then all this is saying in many words what was perfectly said in one sentence in the most felicitous criticism of Maeterlinck ever recorded. The author, oddly enough, was the fair Talulah Bankhead. After watching in rebellious silence for two acts of the perfumed posturing of "Aglyvaine and Selysette," she turned and whispered: "There is *less* in this than meets the eye."

# UNFAMILIAR QUOTATIONS

MME. BORGNY HAMMER, a Scandinavian actress who ventured a few forlorn "Hedda Gabler" matinées at the Little Theater one Winter, appeared the next year to be making a cross-country tour in an Ibsen repertoire, to judge from a descriptive folder wherein I was quoted among other enraptured pressmen, as saying, "Mme. Hammer plays *Hedda* in a majestic . . . manner, her first act recalling . . . Mary Garden's final scene in 'Thais.'" Just why Mme. Hammer should wish it known that her *Hedda* recalled Mary Garden's *Thais*, or, for that matter, anybody's *Thais*, was a matter for speculation. It is barely possible that she thought the comparison would sound well in communities where no *Hedda* and no *Thais* had ever ventured. Perhaps we shall yet live to hear her bashfully quoting someone as having said: "Mme. Hammer plays the *Marchioness* in a high-toned way, her imposing portrait of Dickens's little slavey recalling Clare Eames's *Mary Stuart*."

At all events, the folder came from Staunton, Va., together with an inquiring note from a reader who said:

"Somehow the quotation is not convincing and the enthusiasm shows more restraint than one expects from you.  I shall attend anyhow (one dares miss no entertainment on Main Street), but just for curiosity, won't you tell me what those dots represent?"

I vaguely recalled my motto on that occasion as "Hammer Away" but, after considerable delving in the scrapbook, the dots were traced to the following text, for which there was scarcely room in Mme. Hammer's modest folder.

" No  playwright, living or dead, has suffered such shoddy and generally incompetent reproduction in this country as poor Hendrik Ibsen, and it is really astonishing that the notion that he could write good plays has nevertheless survived to this day.  His most fascinating heroine, *Hedda Gabler*, who will be remembered as having been the victim of a peculiarly painful assault at the Neighborhood Playhouse last year, was given again yesterday afternoon at the Little Theater. The occasion was the first of a series of Ibsen matinées designed as a New York introduction for Mme. Borgny Hammer, who is described in the playbills as hailing from the National Theater of Christiania, though they vouchsafe no further information as to when and in what capacity she adorned that institution.

" *Mme. Hammer plays Hedda in a majestic* and formidable *manner, her first act* costume and recitative *recalling* nothing quite so hauntingly as *Mary Garden's final scene in 'Thais.'* Even the cat-like darts and thrusts of the restless lady she must needs render with a kind of operatic deliberation, so imperfect is her mastery of our tongue. Not that the text thus complicated by her heavily accented speech could by any native actress be made to sound quite natural, so uninspired and uncolloquial is the English translation employed."

Which incident recalls a momentary embarrassment I felt when my loud ballyhoo for that entertaining revival of "Ruddigore," as it was staged and sung at the Park Theater some seasons ago, was later used in behalf of an entirely different production of that blessed opera with which an entirely different organization marched through Georgia. This led to my receiving eleven rude letters from various Georgians.

It also recalls the Homeric laughter which shook the person of Peter Clark Macfarlane when, as he was lecturing across country on the strawberry circuit of the Chautauquas one summer, he came upon the advertising matter of an "Uncle Tom's Cabin" Company working the same territory. Memory does not now retain the number of Topsies and the exact pedigree of the bloodhounds promised by this production, but the folders quoted someone as saying that, all told, it was the most talented and most appropriate company ever

assembled for this celebrated play. And believe it or
not, as you like, this glowing tribute was ascribed in
1921 to no less an authority than Harriet Beecher
Stowe.

Sometimes, when the reviewer is thus misrepresented
he can only grin and bear it. Thus I could hardly
quarrel with Earl Carroll when he chose to quote me as
having described his precious "Bavu" as "an ingenious
melodrama." So read the printed record. As a matter of fact, what I had written was "ingenuous"—a
somewhat different adjective to which all composing
rooms have a deep aversion.

But when Heywood Broun described a certain mori-
bund comedy of New York society life as "a triumph
of dullness and vulgarity" and the ashbarrels immedi-
atley flaunted this incitement, "*A Triumph*"—*Broun
in the Tribune*, he did have cause for quarrel. There we
had a happy example of the old showman's familiar art
of discreet deletion. I experienced another when, in a
rosy glow on a Christmas night, I came raving from one
of George Cohan's new revues. I howled its praises
from the housetops, vowing that never had so gay and
comical a show been given in our town. But, paren-
thetically and just at the end, I did admit, reluctantly,
that it was of, by, and for Broadway and that it would
*not* have a great appeal in the hinterland beyond Columbus Circle. The gratified management sent this tribute
all over the country, altering not a word and omitting

none . . . omitting none, that is, save that one word "not."

There does linger in most theatrical advertisements something of the rosiness of P. T. Barnum's proclamations, and, to an anachronistic degree, something of the essential untrustworthiness of those playbills with which the *Lost Dauphin* and the *Duke of Bilgewater* announced their entertainment down the Mississippi when *Huckleberry Finn* was a boy. The utterly candid announcement is so rare that its occasional appearance in the columns is as startling as a cry in the silent night. No wonder, then, that there was a flutter up and down Broadway one Sunday when the newspapers carried an advertisement of the expiring entertainment at the Vanderbilt, which instead of hinting that it was reluctantly tearing itself away from a devoted and stampeding public admitted frankly enough that it had been a failure. It ran thus:

DESPITE the unanimous and enthusiastic praise bestowed by the press upon LAURETTE TAYLOR for her remarkable performance as Sarah Kantor in FANNIE HURST'S play "HUMORESQUE," the engagement will END NEXT SATURDAY NIGHT OWING TO LACK OF PUBLIC SUPPORT.

Would this candid announcement, one wondered, set a new fashion in theatrical advertisement and lead to the columns reading something like this:

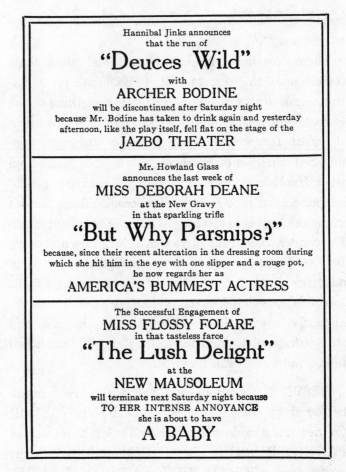

Hannibal Jinks announces
that the run of
## "Deuces Wild"
with
### ARCHER BODINE
will be discontinued after Saturday night
because Mr. Bodine has taken to drink again and yesterday
afternoon, like the play itself, fell flat on the stage of the
### JAZBO THEATER

Mr. Howland Glass
announces the last week of
### MISS DEBORAH DEANE
at the New Gravy
in that sparkling trifle
## "But Why Parsnips?"
because, since their recent altercation in the dressing room during
which she hit him in the eye with one slipper and a rouge pot,
he now regards her as
### AMERICA'S BUMMEST ACTRESS

The Successful Engagement of
### MISS FLOSSY FOLARE
in that tasteless farce
## "The Lush Delight"
at the
### NEW MAUSOLEUM
will terminate next Saturday night because
TO HER INTENSE ANNOYANCE
she is about to have
### A BABY

In the refreshingly frank advertisement which set all
these speculative notions to work one could not help
detecting a note of reproach as though the public
*should* have supported "Humoresque." In that play
Miss Taylor, to my notion, gave the most beautiful

performance of her career in our town, but the play itself was almost unbelievably bad. Those of us who haunt the theater at all times and who are interested in acting as such would wish to see such a performance even in such a play. But the instinct of the everyday playgoer is to stay away. It is a sound instinct. At all events, Miss Hurst would have to say, with *Cassius*, "The fault, dear *Brutus*, is not in our stars, but in ourselves."

Of course the announcement sarcastic is not new. It was during a meagerly attended Shakespearean engagement in Philadelphia that the advertisements ran something like this: "Mr. Richard Mansfield is sorry to disturb the inhabitants of Philadelphia, but he is playing 'Richard III.' every night at the Walnut Street Theater."

Then there was that surprising advertisement which George C. Tyler inserted in the newspapers the first Sunday after a production of his had been exhibited in New York and been treated to a brick shower by all the reviewers of the town. The advertisement ran something like this:

THE NOTORIOUSLY BAD ACTOR
GEORGE ARLISS
in a new play on that hackneyed theme, Americanism
**"Poldekin"**
by the well known hack-writer
BOOTH TARKINGTON

There is a legend along Broadway which would have it that, before many hours had elapsed, Mr. Tyler received two written comments on this japery of his, one from each of the artists whose name he had taken in vain. One of them was couched in language of wounded dignity, implying that Mr. Tyler would never be forgiven as long as the writer lived. The other was just a roaring report on how that advertisement had made this second writer laugh all day long. Now which was from Mr. Arliss and which from Mr. Tarkington is just one of those things we shall not be told until, shortly before the Day of Judgment, Mr. Tyler publishes his memoirs. Of course there is no law against your guessing.

# THE SPEAKER OF THE EVENING

Of all the fine gestures of our time, none satisfied me so completely as one which legend credits to the Rev. M. Woolsey Stryker who was president in what, for some reason, I always think of as the Golden Age of Hamilton College. It was a gesture he made at the end of a week in which the city of Utica, New York, had been glutted with oratory. They were dedicating a church there and the services lasted eight days. On the eighth day—the second Sunday, it was—there were to be three speakers. The third was Dr. Stryker, as superb an orator as I have ever heard.

In the moment before this final service, the three speakers of the day converged in the vestry and it was Dr. Stryker himself who took the precaution to propose that each of them be limited to twenty minutes. It had been the genial presiding clergyman's idea to let them ramble on indefinitely but, as the one who would have to sit through the other two, Dr. Stryker was firm and the twenty minute limitation was agreed upon and the three filed to the platform.

Dr. Stryker settled into his seat and listened. The

235

first man spoke. He spoke only thirty minutes. There was a restless flutter in the church. The second man spoke. He spoke for one hour and a half, and sat down happy in the consciousness of having given good measure. There was an anxious pause. Dr. Stryker walked forward. He looked coldly at his predecessors. He looked compassionately on the wilted rows before him.

"This congregation," he said gently, "looks very much dedicated. So I will say nothing to you Uticans beyond suggesting that you all go home now and read that chapter in the New Testament which tells how Paul preached all night and Eutychus fell out of the window."

Once I sat listening at a dedication when the three speakers were Mayor Hylan of New York, Governor Miller of New York and President Harding and, when any one of the three was speaking, it was not difficult to guess from the expression of the other two that they were wondering why he was talking so long—a state of mind which deserted each of them when he rose himself to speak.

With a single exception, I have never enjoyed one of the several hundred banquets I have been obliged to attend. I have never squirmed through the speaking without wondering why in the name of common sense dinner committees still labored under the delusion that anyone ever wanted anyone to speak. Yet, when I myself am invited to speak, nothing can keep me at home.

The most entertaining after dinner speech I ever heard was one given by Father Duffy. The most admirable was another by Franklin P. Adams who, when roguishly asked by the toastmaster if, after all the promises that he would not be called upon, he did not still wish to say just a few informal words to the old Michigan grads, he rose, looked about him, said one word and sat down. The one word was "No."

Almost the most gratifying climax in modern dramatic literature is that which comes at the end of one of the "Diminutive Dramas" by Maurice Baring. The scene is a town near Rome, the occasion the dedication of a bridge and the climax comes when, after ages of local oratory, Caligula lifts a lazy jeweled hand as a signal to his soldiery to charge forward and pitch everyone present into the Tiber. And quite right, too.

All of these morose reflections followed after the most prodigiously dull dinner of my experience—a banquet served to mark the fourth birthday of the Theater Guild. It seems probable that the three or four hundred reasonably constant lovers of the drama who were turned away from the Waldorf that night because there was not another inch of room for them, went about town the next day grinning thankfully from ear to ear. Their original yearning to attend was doubtless based on the assumption that the resourceful young directors

of the guild could be counted on to arrange post-
prandial revels of a piquant, or at least an untra-
ditional, kind. They were wrong—completely, grotesquely, wrong. By the next afternoon they probably
knew it. By that time the 1,500 who did attend, or
at least the considerably smaller number who remained doggedly to the end, must have roused themselves sufficiently to stand up and admit that they
had been decoyed into attending the dullest, the most
incredibly unimaginative, tedious and stodgy dinner in
the history of the long suffering Waldorf. The guild,
which can produce Shaw and Milne and even Ibsen
without turning a hair, cannot produce a dinner. Its
first attempt, this jolly little celebration of the guild's
fourth birthday, would have been resented even if it had
been put forth as a Kiwanis Club luncheon in Utica, as
a Rotary Club banquet in Buffalo or as one of those
dear, exhausting, old dinners they hold at commencement
time at Hamilton College. And oddly enough this func-
tion was seriously intended as the opening gun in a campaign to raise half a million dollars for a new theater.
In other words this campaign was launched by luring
1,500 of the guild's heartiest and most dependable
friends into one room and boring them to tears.

Waiving for a moment the moot question as to how
many people ever really want to hear anyone, however
eloquent, make a speech at all, it will be generally agreed
that few people wish to sit on dinky gold chairs and

listen to thirteen speakers. And surely nobody in all this world wants to sit in such a room, on such a chair, and listen to two hours and fifteen minutes of rambling remarks. Yet such was the entertainment (*snarls and sarcastic laughter*), such was the giddy revel planned by the guild's dinner committee. The toastmaster was the adroit and undismayed Frank Crowninshield, editor extraordinary of *Vanity Fair*. The speakers involved were Heywood Broun, Walter Prichard Eaton, John Corbin, Constantin Stanislavsky, Walter Lippmann, Mrs. August Belmont, Theresa Helburn, Philip Moeller, Lee Simonson, Maurice Wertheim, Lawrence Langner and one ink-stained wretch who has asked that his name be suppressed.

Beginning with Mr. Broun, who said a few graceful things of no special import and fled craftily into the night, the speaking was well launched at 10 o'clock. By 11 it was at its height. Here and there, to be sure, the surface of the assemblage was eddying with little knots of people who were rising and stealing toward the door. By 11:15 the exodus was more marked. By 11:30 they were running, not walking, to the nearest exits. By a quarter to 12 the gaps in the audience made the room look like an old comb with half its teeth gone. The faithful remainder sat weary, wilted, their yawns breaking from control, their eyes turning glassy in their grim determination not to let them close in slumber. Women began to shift their hairpins and to

grope with their feet for slippers that had escaped.
When midnight came and went some were so stunned
that when it was all over they didn't believe it.  Friends
had to prod them into rising and going home.

In behalf of the fugitive Mr. Crowninshield, it was
explained to the posse of indignant citizens who went to
look for him after the dispersal that he had not been responsible for the number of incorrigible speakers who
had been invited to the dinner.  He could not even be
blamed, said they, for the fellows who were asked to
speak two minutes and light heartedly spoke twelve.
And indeed there was a wistful look about Mr. Crowninshield all through his dreadful ordeal.

We were reminded of the predicament which once
faced Burr McIntosh (recently billed in a perplexing
fashion as "America's Own Burr McIntosh").  He was
master of ceremonies at one of those scandalous benefit performances at the Manhattan, where none of the
advertised stars appeared and before each number he
had to come before a stony audience and announce a
substitute unknown to fame.  And each time he rubbed
his hands and beamed and said:  "Now I am going to
announce a great big splendid *surprise*."  Thus Mr.
Crowninshield looking out over a restless, resentful
audience of which a goodly proportion was frankly in
full retreat, would say in a voice almost convincing: "We
are fortunate in having with us to-night the delightful and
astounding Mr. Gazump, secretary of the Better Drama

Group of Cohoes, who will, I hope, consent to address us." Trust Mr. Gazump. Indeed, not once in all the evening did any one of the Gazumps have the simple dignity and common sense to rise and say: "Not on your life!" and sit down. That obvious gesture lay open to all the last half dozen speakers. Yet, directed from within by a kind of poltroonery and possibly, also, by a secret sneaking vanity which told him that he, after all, was the one they all really wanted to hear, not one of them made that gesture. It was too bad, as the guild really deserved a new theater, and it seemed grossly improbable that any of the 1,500 would relent and buy a bond.

# THE PASSING OF THE THANATOPSIS

THE Thanatopsis—less frequently but more accurately known as the Young Men's Upper West Side Thanatopsis and Inside Straight Club—is no more. At least, I suppose it isn't. Three of its most reliable members—Heywood Broun, Marc Connelly and I—handed in our resignations in the Fall of 1923, and it seems hardly probable that the remaining ten or twelve members are still forlornly holding the meetings every Saturday evening.

We resigned because poker (with just three final rounds of jackpots, everybody up, at nine o'clock in the morning) is a preposterous waste of time. That's what we say—a waste of time. The persistent rumors that we resigned from pique at our losses are unworthy of those who circulate them. It just happens to be true that Mr. Connelly (as always) and Mr. Broun and myself, for a change, did suffer some rather severe misfortunes; but, as we always say, it all evens up in the course of a year. To be sure, *George Osborne* said the same thing to *Dobbin* as long ago as the pre-Waterloo chapters of *Vanity Fair*, but it's still as true as ever. Just about.

No, our objection to poker is that it's a waste of time. Just what we will do with the time thus saved has not yet been definitely decided. Broun is doubtless writing a few novels, or planning to. I remember his first announcing his contract to write "The Boy Grew Older." I might (and, in fact, will) add that it was at a birthday dinner of mine when he explained that it was to be done in a few months. That careful craftsman, Alice Duer Miller, knowing how much other work he had on hand, protested that he would not have time. "Well," muttered Broun doggedly, "I'm not very busy Friday afternoons."

Connelly, I imagine, has reverted to rum at the Players' Club (the game, not the potion), and I spend the quiet evenings alone with my books.

It was more than the mere waste of time that led to our resignation from the Thanatopsis Club. Some of the finer fibered members had been feeling for some time that, beneath its surface jollity and cameraderie, there was brewing a distinct animosity. We had all been very good friends at the start, and most of us were still speaking. But hardly a member had been adroitly called home when he was several hundred dollars ahead, who was not sped on his way by the hearty hope of all his pals that he would fall down and break his neck. Indeed, the only brother who enjoyed the unbroken good will of the fraternity was Brother Marc Connelly, whose charming, childlike and quite incurable curiosity as to what the other guy might be holding made him an invariable loser. In fact, there were many weeks when his royalty checks from "Merton of the Movies" and "To the Ladies" were laughingly divided every Saturday evening among his cronies of the Thanatopsis, who voted him a jolly good fellow, you may be sure.

Other jolly good fellows, at one time or another, have been Jerome Kern, who is a *good* composer; Robert E. Sherwood, the bitter movie critic who, unfortunately, became extremely married; Montague Glass, cautious but dependable; John V. A. Weaver, who lost in one perfectly delightful afternoon the entire royalties of "In American" for the preceding six months, and so had to sort of eat around for some time; Donald Ogden Stewart, who, at poker, is even funnier than in his books; and, bless his heart, Prince Antoine Bibesco, the engaging Minister at Washington from Roumania. Another was the permanent Infant Phenomenon of American letters, F. Scott Fitzgerald, whose jollity, it is true, was somewhat complicated by his passion for pausing in the midst of his deal to do some of the cutest card tricks you ever saw.

In all honesty, I cannot keep up a pretense that all the casual visitors to the Thanatopsis were jolly good fellows. As I recall, William Slavens McNutt proved hopeless when regarded as a victim. And Haldemann-Julius, that snappy publisher out Kansas way, who is always breaking out like a rash in the magazines with his positively last, final offer to send you, postpaid, an entire set of Oscar Wilde for five cents—Haldemann-Julius left none of his profits with his hosts.

Nor did the only two women who have ever been tolerated in the game prove to be either so jolly or so good as we could have wished. Indeed, both Neysa McMein and Mrs. Raoul Fleischmann (known to the Middle Western press as "Quincy's talented daughter" and "Quincy's untalented daughter," respectively) —both of these fair visitors played shrewdly, pocketed their winnings, and refused ever ̩to sit in the game again on the grounds that the stakes were too high.

Then there was that least jolly fellow of them all—a certain rich man who was brought in one night by a sponsor, who explained that he would be almost *too* easy. Next day we looked the fellow up in Dun and Bradstreet, which gave his fortune as $60,000,000. We wrote that excellent bureau a little note.

"Dear Sirs": we said, "He now has $60,000,210."

The passing of Prince Bibesco caused a mild hilarity in the Thanatopsis. His seeming unawareness of what was going on led to the friendliest welcome being accorded him. With a delicate accent that is simply unreproducible in type, he would inquire in the midst of a painful pot: "Does the—what do you call them? I forget. Oh, yes—does a sequence excel in competition with three facials?"

"He probably means," someone would explain gruffly, "does a straight beat three kings?"

But when it began to dawn on the guileless Thanatopsis that the Prince knew full well what a straight would beat, and that, as a matter of fact, he was beaming at the time on a brave but busted flush, a dark suspicion was born among the members that Balkan diplomacy was lifting its ugly head in their innocent revels. It was found, to be sure, that one could get even with the Prince by referring to his game as "funny without being Bulgar," or by pretending to confuse Roumania with Serbia. But on one occasion he achieved a feat in poker so excruciating that these minor reprisals were felt to be inadequate. Then was Herbert Bayard Swope, the thunderous editor of the *World*, inspired to an immortal dismissal.

"Boy," he cried to the nearest flunkey, "boy, the Prince's hat and cuffs!"

But, as I have said, it gradually became apparent that poker was undermining the amiability of even the most equable members; that its acid was corroding the oldest friendships. For instance, this must have dawned on Henry Wise Miller one evening. (Mr. Miller is the only member of the Thanatopsis who is in trade, being literary only by marriage. He represents Alice Duer Miller at the meetings, for her only game is cribbage, and she is no whiz at that.) One evening, Brother Miller stepped outside to spank his automobile,

or whatever it is that motorists do to their cars when
they step outside to look at them. Even as he stepped,
on this occasion, he cried for help. There, half way down
the street, a gang of larcenous thugs were struggling
with the locked machine.

"Ah, moi!" cried Miller, in his admirable French.
Now if, on that evening, he had been a jolly good fellow—but his brothers just looked at the preposterous,
hoarded mass of chips from which he had been thriftily
investing as the game waned. They looked at it and
grinned.

"Ah, moi!" The voice of Miller sounded fainter and
fainter down the block.

"I open it," said F. P. A. "I open it for $13.50."

The same suspicion of unfriendliness must have
dawned, too, on the usually successful and not at all
jolly Heywood Broun that Fall when, after losing $250
one night at the Thanatopsis, he went into the country
for a rest and, amid somewhat complicated pastoral
scenes, next night lost $850 more. Thus one week-end
had cost him a sum which, if properly invested, would,
in time, have provided two much needed years at
Hamilton College for H. 3rd.

Yet, when he came plaintively back to town and told
his story to the brethren, they did not say, "Heywood,
draw on me for anything you may need." They did not
say, "Tough luck, old fellow," nor silently press his
hand in the quiet way of strong men. Not they. They

did, in fact, none of these things. Without exception, his pals almost died laughing.

The aforesaid suspicion certainly ate into the heart of John Peter Toohey, the author of "Fresh Every Hour," who gave the Thanatopsis its name and is usually addressed as "Our dear founder." One night he arrived late at the game, explaining with difficulty that he had had the hiccoughs for forty-eight hours and might die if anyone held three aces on him. Everyone laughed heartily and there was only immense good humor when, from time to time, our founder would withdraw to the hall and do something to himself that seemd to help for a while. But finally he grew desperate.

"I have heard," he said, "that a last resort is to stand on your head. I am afraid that I shall have to ask two of you gentlemen to hold my feet." But this intrinsically entertaining appeal came at a time when the game was growing haggard and when the winners, at the slightest interruption, would seize the chance to slip off home to the wife and kiddies—the dirty crooks. "I am afraid—," our founder began again, but no one was listening.

At last, when the game did dissolve, two brothers agreed to drop Toohey at the Presbyterian Hospital on their way home, inasmuch as they would be passing it anyway. But, by this time, he was so discouraged about the human race that a nervous panic seized him when he found it would be necessary to wake the night nurse. Indeed, he was so alarmed at the way she would take his interruption of her slumbers that when she did come drowsily down, the hiccoughs had been scared out of him, and have not recurred since.

Those of us who have now withdrawn from this corroding atmosphere cannot be missing so very much after all. The famous banter of the Thanatopsis, the wit which was supposed to glance dazzlingly off its stacks of chips, has been grossly exaggerated and, under present conditions, must, I think, be pretty forlorn.

To be sure, George S. Kaufman has been known to lift the general average by occasional contributions, as when he upset the club's gravity one evening by observing casually that he was descended from old Sir Roderick Kaufman, who went on the crusades. Fourteen eye-brows rose in well bred surprise, and Kaufman added, hastily, "as a spy."

But, for the most part, the Thanatopsis jokes have become routine; and I, for one, shall not greatly miss hearing Kaufman, every time he holds an ace and a nine, say he is going to make an ace-nine bet. Or every time he has a two in the hole and a three is dealt him, hearing him complain bitterly that he is being tray-deuced.

I was amused enough when, on the night I forgot to bring a promised liqueur to the game, Mr. Broun offered to go back to my house for it. He would always, he said, be glad to walk a mile for a kümmel. But I grew rather tired of his little joke about the port he always served on rainy nights.  It was a second rate rabbinical beverage; but, as Broun used to say, with a fatuous delight in his own (I suppose it was his own) wit, "Any port in a storm."

I shall not even miss the singing.  There was the song which escaped into the outer world through the medium of F. P. A.'s column.  It ran something like this:

> "Oh, Mr. Connelly, oh, Mr. Connelly,
>     I'll wager thirty dollars on this hand;
>         I think its pretty fair,
>         Perhaps I have a pair;
> Have you got thirty bucks at your command?"

> "Oh, Mr. Broun, oh, Mr. Broun,
>     I'll call you, for I think you are a loon.
>         As upon your hand I gaze,
>         I see just a pair of trays."
>     "What have you got, Mr. Connelly?"
>     "A pair of sevens, Mr. Broun."

Far more inspiring, to be sure, both musically and lyrically, was the club's own anthem, a stirring chant, sung standing by every member except the one who had just made a fool call.  The melody was that of the Bosun's song in "Pinafore," and the magnificent refrain was:

> "He remains a God damned fool."

No, the delights of the Thanatopsis were not sufficient to outweigh its evils. Thus, a club that was formed on the Butte Montmartre during the war, passes into history. It was started there by Harold W. Ross, a buck private who was editor of the *Stars and Stripes* and who, at Nini's little hole-in-the-wall near the Place du Tertre, used to show a good time to the sundry lieutenants who would come up to Paris for a week's leave and who, sometimes, departed despondently for their outfits the second day. (Ask one of them who is now in the faculty at Johns Hopkins.) Back in New York, this game gradually took form as the weekly Thanatopsis. Now that, too, has passed. Or at least, I suppose it has. Though, immediately on hearing me use the word "pass," some officious zany may have opened it.

# BON VOYAGE

THERE is no routine kindness more annoying than the *bon voyage* gift. It is astonishing with what regularity your friends can select a little something for which you could have no possible use at sea or a big something for which you could find no room at all in your luggage.

A basket of fruit or a good book—that is the form it usually takes. The trouble with the fruit is that you never quite know what to do with it. It may seem a little unappreciative to send it at once to the steerage, or, just as the ship glides past Ambrose, to open your porthole and pitch it furtively into the sea. Yet if you leave it in your stateroom you find half your voyage intolerably complicated by the strange aromatics of decay. Of course you cannot possibly eat the stuff. You need all your capacity to meet the emergency involved in each of the six meals wherewith the chief steward strives to keep the passengers distracted.

A book, too, is a doubtful blessing. You are wont to find yourself sailing off in quest of adventure, as I did one summer, weighted down with four copies of "Gentle Julia." Besides, it is an illusion, hotly denied by all ex-

252

perience, that you want to read much—or at any rate, that you *will* read much while on shipboard. If you do, there is the ship's library, and as the voyage is nearly over before you can lure the deck steward into opening the cases in the salon, it does not much matter that the old bookworm who made the collection for the ship owners was the kind that would select a set of the complete works of Beaumarchais in superb bindings and terrible type, several books of about the weight and vintage of "The Mississippi Bubble" by Emerson Hough, and an excessive number of hymnals. It does not much matter because by this time enough people will have begun to leave really alluring books on their deck chairs while grimly taking their constitutionals, and if you are careful to study the periodicity of their recurrence on your side of the ship you can collect quite a little traveling library and keep it in your stateroom.

Some *bon voyage* gifts that seem so charming while the good-bys are still being waved from the pier are likely to lose their glamour before the trip is over. I was once thus deceived by the tribute of a lot of jolly friends who came down to see me off. It was in the lax, pre-war days when one's pals could swarm up the gang plank, examine my stateroom and laugh heartily at its dimensions. On this occasion so many bottles of champagne were ordered up and quaffed with good wishes that I sailed across warmed by the glow of a true illusion of popularity. This was not dispelled until we reached

Liverpool and I was forbidden to land until I had settled for the champagne.

But after all, these facetious experiments are merely commendable efforts to escape from the iron routine of fruit baskets and just a few good books. That was really the kindly spirit which animated some of my playmates one Spring when they merrily packed my stateroom with children's toys—blocks, geography games, drawing slates and everything a not particularly bright lad of eight could desire. The same rogues sped Reinald Werrenrath on his overseas concert tour by sending him two parrots to the ship.

Having all these precedents in mind and resolute not to indulge in that ancient jest of sending goldfish, —it was to Charles Hanson Towne as he boarded a train to Chicago one afternoon long ago that some roguish friends presented a bowl of goldfish—I tried hard on one occasion, when a whole family was going right out of my life, to think of a *bon voyage* gift that no one had ever given before and that really would amuse or please the voyagers. After much cogitation I compiled a tantalizing questionnaire, with sealed answers, to be opened only at the end of the voyage. Take these home and try them on your culture:

    1.  To whom was Jane Eyre dedicated?

    2.  What famous Irishman eked out a precarious income in his youth by flute playing on the Continent?

3. Name three modern playwrights who started out as physicians?

4. Where was Richard Mansfield born?

5. What was the origin and first significance of the Italian word for "German"—tedesco?

6. Who was Brooks of Sheffield?

7. Who wrote the letters of Junius?

8. What common phrase, made of French words, is never heard in France or seen in a French dictionary?

9. What celebrated English novel of our day was published posthumously?

10. In diplomacy what is the difference between an identic and an identical note?

11. The plot of what famous English novel was offered to Henry James as a gift?

12. Who was the Bisley Boy?

13. What is the Wicked Bible?

14. Who was the original of *Horace Skimpole* in "Bleak House?"

15. What was Voltaire's real name?

16. What poet was an onlooker at the Battle of Valmy?

17. What Shakespearian play has the greatest preponderance of verse?

18. Name two famous European authors who had negro blood in their veins?

19. What celebrated literary romance resulted from a chance confrontation at Avignon?

20.   What great Austrian on his death-bed besought his friends to send him the works of Fenimore Cooper?

Such a gift can be prepared for about seven cents, including paper, stamps, and wear and tear on your reference books.   Readers wishing to make such a gift should be cautioned, however, to offer it to someone who is leaving the country.   Do not, under any circumstances, deliver it by hand.   If you do the gratified recipient will glance it over, admit genially that he can answer only two or three, and then, turning radiant on you, will ask severely:  "Can you name three modern Chinese poets?"

# DE SENECTUTE

THE other day an uncommonly decorative girl of twenty shocked me. It was my fault for having tried idly to find out why her usual sunlit loveliness was overcast with the visible and unaccustomed processes of thought. It seemed, according to an explanation vouchsafed from behind a brow still prettily furrowed, that she was poised uncertain between two proposals of marriage. One was from a rich and cleanly architect, who wished her to be his at her earliest convenience, but she could not quite make up her mind to accept him. "Do you love him?" I asked in my orthodox way. "Love him!" she exclaimed in wondering accents. "Why, I dislike him."

However, that was not the shock. The shock came in her instinctive recoil from the loathsome alternative. It was a handsome offer from one who she described in her own quaint language as "an old sweetie." She was, one gathered, just too fond of him for words, and he of her. But, after all, should a young girl let herself become an old man's darling? "Who," I asked, though it would have been better had I let the matter

257

drop, "is this senile admirer?" "I won't tell you his name," she went on, lifting, in her charming perplexity, the eyes of a wounded angel. "Besides, he isn't feeble or anything like that. But he's every day of thirty-six."

It is pure, unstudied judgments like that which make a man think. Especially when he is just thirty-six. Here am I, for instance, a slippered pantaloon slinking toward a thirty-seventh birthday—a doddering scribbler driven at last to the conclusion, not only that I don't amount to much but that I never will. I might as well face the fact that I never have written anything and never will write anything that will live after me. It's rather sad, when you look at it that way.

And yet—well, at least there are some things I HAVEN'T written. Couldn't an epitaph be wrought for me on that basis? Would it not be better for me to rest my case on the strength of the things I never did? In the obituary in my home-town paper, let them say this of me:

He never wrote the word "anent."

He never, never called children "the kiddies."

When he wanted to say: "But that's another story," he did not feel impelled to add: "As Kipling would have said."

He wrote thousands of dramatic criticisms and never once used the word "personality."

He never wrote "so to speak."

He never used the phrase "as it were."

He contrived a thousand newspaper headlines and never once replaced "Them" by "'Em" under the impression that that made the headline funny.

When wishing to say that "Ethan Frome" was the best short story ever written by an American or that "The Greek Commonwealth" was the best historical work ever written anywhere, he never sneaked in a "probably" or a "perhaps" under the delusion that in some way it would give him a judicious air or a suggestion of profundity.

He never strung a number of play titles together under the delusion that there was something ingenuous and highly comical about such a sentence as this: "The Swan" sang "The Lullaby" in the "Rain" until "Abie's Irish Rose" became a "Nervous Wreck."

He never sent *Life* a joke about the difference between a pessimist and an optimist.

He wrote three hundred thousand words about the war without using the word "comrades" or the phrase "supreme sacrifice."

He once wrote an article about Maude Adams and Barrie in which neither the word "charm" nor the word "whimsical" occurred.

He never used the phrase "The uselessness of it all."

In quoting such a line as "But, oh, the difference to me!" he would not add: "as the poet—was it Wordsworth?—so beautifully phrases it." Not when he knew doggone well it was Wordsworth and had, in fact, just looked it up in Bartlett.

All in all, he wasn't a bad chap.

May his soul rest in peace.